ESSENTIAL CHINESE MYTHOLOGY

Essential Chinese Mythology

STORIES THAT CHANGE THE WORLD

MARTIN PALMER AND ZHAO XIAOMIN
WITH JOANNE O'BRIEN AND JAMES PALMER

Thorsons
An Imprint of HarperCollins*Publishers*

In loving thanks to all those who taught us how to tell stories,
but most especially to Rosemary Sutcliffe

Thorsons
An Imprint of HarperCollins*Publishers*
77–85 Fulham Palace Road
Hammersmith, London W6 8JB
1160 Battery Street
San Francisco, California 94111–1213

First published by Thorsons 1997

3 5 7 9 10 8 6 4 2

Martin Palmer and Zhao Xiaomin assert the moral right to
be identified as the authors of this work

A catalogue record for this book is available from the
British Library

ISBN 1 85538 476 0

Printed and bound in Great Britain by
Caledonian International Book Manufacturing Ltd, Glasgow

Contents

Introduction: Unravelling the myths

There is a problem in understanding Chinese mythology in that we tend to use the singular form of the word 'mythology'. For in reality there is no Chinese mythology as such, but there are innumerable mythologies. There are at least two major contemporary strands – Taoist and Buddhist – as well as a third which fuses elements of both. Behind these mythologies there lies a host of more ancient mythologies stretching back to the mists of time, and handed down from the many hundreds of different tribes in scores of regions of China. Added to this is the attempt to standardize and cleanse mythology undertaken by the great Confucian writers, historians and philosophers, as well as the modern mythologies of the Nationalist and Communist regimes.

We have tried to reflect this variety by examining different clusters of myths. Although they have an inner logic provided by, for example, Buddhism, they often seem to have no direct relationship to other clusters of myths such as the origin stories.

It is important to recall quite how vast and diverse China is – one quarter of the world's population, numerous different tribes and groupings, vastly different cultures, and enormous expanses of land and water. China is not, for all that its rulers have sometimes wanted it to be, a unified culture. Even under the harshest of modern regimes, that of the Communist Party, fifty-three different nationalities or groupings are officially recognized. But the reality is far wider than that – China is a mosaic of diverse groups and of multitudes of traditions. There are of course elements which transcend and even unite many of these different aspects, but there is as much which divides and differentiates.

When we speak of Chinese mythology we need to be clear that it represents streams flowing together, running parallel, merging or diverging from many places and from many different models of reality. This is why I prefer to speak of Chinese mythologies.

Let me give two examples of this process.

In the sixth century BC, China was divided into ten states, many of which were bigger than states in modern day Europe. These states each had their own myths of foundation; their own clan heroes, their own prominent deities, their own divine protectors. They had their own histories, their lineage of power to their kings, their own rituals and practices. Gradually, as the number of kingdoms declined through the aggrandisement of a few of the larger states, these traditions were absorbed or displaced by those of the conquerors' own. Eventually, all these kingdoms were suppressed and the first true Empire of China emerged in 221 BC under the brutal but brilliant dynasty of the Chin.

One of the most infamous actions of that dynasty was the burning of the books. The ruler, Chin Shih Huang Ti, whose terracotta warriors have just been unearthed near Xian, realized that if people could read of former and different times, then they would always have alternative models of reality by which to challenge his claim to absolute power. But destroy the knowledge that life could be lived in any other way than under a police state dictatorship and people would be your captives.

In doing this, the First Emperor of historical China was simply taking to its logical conclusion something that Confucian scholars had already been undertaking – namely the rewriting of the past to make it serve the present and future. We have no way of knowing what riches of mythology were lost by such actions or which were lost as China progressively unified and standardized. It is inevitable that much was lost, for ancient traditions and lineages died out or were snuffed out, and with them went the knowledge and the focus for many such myths. What was allowed to remain at the official level was either what was seen as useful to those in power or that which could manage to integrate itself into the new theocracies and hierarchies of the divine which the conquering or dominant group brought. The fact is that much continued to be retained of the older myths, through folk legends, stories associated with a particular sacred site, or through re-emergence in a new form.

The second example I want to give is the extraordinary elements which went into the making of the story of Wen Cheng, the god of Literature whose full story is given on pages 95–9. In brief, this god combines a tribal thundergod, a clan/kingdom protector deity, an astrological dimension, Confucian virtues and values, Taoist immortality narratives, avatar stories, cosmological dimensions and popular fortune-telling. The confusion of images and data contained in the stories which create Wen Cheng is so great that when Emperor Jen Tsung (of the early 14th century) officially raised the god to the status of Benevolent Emperor, the official edict publicly acknowledged the confusing nature of the stories of the god and simply accepted this as part and parcel of divine reality!

To understand Chinese mythologies, we need to treat the whole adventure of the rise of these mythologies as a narrative in its own right. To start, we have to go right back to the earliest times and we need to begin by getting rid of one major preoccupation of Western mythology: the desire to find a creation myth.

3

The Earliest Myths of China

The earliest myths of China, or to be even more precise of those peoples who came to live in China, contain no discernible creation stories. Creation stories as such are quite late developments in mythologies. The creation stories in the Bible, in Genesis, are amongst the last things written down in the chronological development of the Hebrew Bible/Old Testament. For most tribal or indigenous peoples, creation is not an issue. What is an issue is how they got to be in that particular part of the world, or where they came from, or how they began to establish their own identity. Speculation about original causes is a much later philosophical advance, as is clear in China.

The earliest myths we have relate to heroes who become divine – a feature of much of Chinese mythology – and of how certain things came into being. These stories take us back to perhaps 900 BC in written form or to earlier than that in oral form. They are fragments or hints, nothing more. China never had a Homer to rewrite its core myths in popular fashion nor has it produced sacred books concerned primarily with telling the stories of the gods. Those which we can turn to are very late developments – dating in the most part from the mid to late Ming, around 1500 – 1600 AD. Where myths survive they do so as incidentals in histories or in accounts of travel or in philosophical speculation or as the back drop to dramas. Because there was no one great collector or refiner of the myths of China in antiquity, there was no point at which they were aligned and gaps filled, which is what happened with the Biblical myths when the need for a Creation story was discovered.

Instead they deal with questions such as: Where did writing come from? How did our ancestors learn to plough, weave, sow?

Who taught us to cook and to build houses? Who was our founding father and mother? They are often aetiological – that is ascribing meaning set in the past to current practices or to sacred sites.

An example of an aetiological story is related to the most sacred of the sacred mountains of China – T'ai Shan. This massive mountain, rising from the flat plains on the coastal edge of northern China, has obviously been a centre for religious practices for millennia. Its origins lie back in shamanistic pre-history. The earliest stone inscription, from the Han period, shows that people came to the mountain to pray for help and blessings.

When the cult of Emperors was instituted, most noticeably by the same Chin Shih Huang Ti mentioned above, a shrine of origin was needed. Chin Shih Huang Ti had burst beyond the confines of his original ancestor myths for he had long ago conquered territories which took him away from his ancestral home and into new pastures. He needed a new mythology of power and right to rule. He also wished to show, as Alexander the Great did when, upon conquering Egypt, he claimed that he was a son of the Egyptian gods, that he was blessed by the old gods. So he took himself to T'ai Shan to worship at the site where, mythology had it, the Mother and Father of Heaven had lived. Thus he could take the title of Son of Heaven. Unfortunately for him, his first visit coincided with a violent thunder storm, which was taken to show the gods' displeasure, thereby undercutting the power he had sought to gain by hijacking the symbolism.

To this day, the desire to make Chinese mythology serve the notion of a unified, ideologically sound, present-day China continues. Penguin recently published a translation of a book published in China on Chinese mythology, in association with the Foreign Language Press, Beijing. The author, Yuan Ke, is obviously writing as a Marxist concerned to make mythology useful to present-day political China. Thus he has four categories which, while having some general relevance, are all given a Marxist slant to make them acceptable to the present regime. Thus he talks about 'Praising labour'. 'Admiring the relentless spirit of heroes.' 'Glorifying the common people's resistance to dictatorial rule.' 'Describing the people's longing for love, freedom of marriage and a happy family life.'

What the above stories show is that what we have left in the records of mythology is what has been through the refining fire of time, dynastic politics and ancient forms of political correctness. It is therefore very hard indeed to know what the earliest people thought. For the earliest myths there are only a few primary sources. The three most important sources are the Shih Ching, the Classic of Poetry which contains material from the Chou dynasty onwards; the Songs of the South, shamanistic poems and epics of the Chou people, recorded in writing around 450 BC, and the early Han dynasty book, from roughly 200 BC, The Classic of the Mountains and the Seas – a sort of encyclopaedia of folk knowledge. From these three sources, bits and pieces can be found of ancient myths. But often what we are given is nothing more than a hint of a story that has now completely disappeared. Most of this material is not systematic, but of an anecdotal nature, just cropping up when the writers in the Shih Ching or the Classic happen to need to refer to them.

Yet we can see from other writings, particularly by philosophers such as Chuang Tzu, that they moved in a world rich with mythology and mythologized history – of which more later. Chuang Tzu intermingles heroic figures from mytho-history – such as Yi the Archer, the founder father of the Chou tribes, and filial and virtuous rulers such as Shun, with gods and deities such as the Kuei monster or Fu Hsi, the snake-man bringer of civilization.

In other words, we cannot really talk convincingly of recovering much of the mythologies of the peoples of China prior to the creation of a written record, kept and purified by different interest groups. Of these the strongest and most long lasting were the scholar historians, almost all Confucian, who served the interests of the dynasties from the Chou (221 – 206 BC) onwards.

In terms of what we know of early Chinese mythologies, we have to rely upon scraps of information, preserved more by accident than by design, in materials which usually had a didactic rather than a narrative function. There are various reasons why a Confucian scholar or historian might preserve a fragment of a story about an early deity of China; perhaps they are using such a person as a model of Confucian values or to explain a folk custom or the name of a particular area. In other words, the fragment is retained because it is used to highlight something considered of value by the writer. That this usually had nothing whatever to do with the ordinary function served by the myth in its own time can be deduced from the fact that even when purged for use as an exemplar, odd bits of inconsistent history still cling to the fragment. For example, the figures Fu Hsi and Nu Kua are able to be both human and animal in form, and the accounts of Kun and Yu show their ability to turn into bears, thus the shamanistic roots of these figures have been preserved.

Heroes of the ancient past

If gods and their narratives were going to survive at all it was either by being cleaned up or by persisting in oral and folk tradition, where they inevitably underwent changes as the fashions of narrative and models of divinity changed.

To illustrate this cleaning-up process we need only look at what happened to the extraordinarily complex collection of founder figures in the earliest mythological traditions of China.

When the Confucian historians came to chart the prehistory of China they had two enormous problems. The first was that Kung Fu Tzu himself – best known in the West by the Latinised version of his name, Confucius – had proclaimed that the Emperors of old were models of virtue; exemplars of filial and virtuous conduct; ministers of great benevolence and righteousness. Thus the historians had to look at the ancient past through what can only be described as rose tinted glasses. In the distant past all the Emperors were good; all the rulers were thoughtful; all the ministers pillars of propriety. Those that were not were manifestly evil, scheming and bad. Kung Fu Tzu had romanticized the ancient past to the point of making it incapable of holding the real ambiguity and plurality of the mythic past of China. The end result was that a host of deities, heroes and villains were marshalled into line in order to prove that there were Emperors and rulers of the fiction called China and that they had ruled in ways of such righteousness and benevolence as to put to shame the current rulers of the day, each lording it over a separate kingdom instead of over a united China. The myths were used for almost purely didactic purposes.

This is where the fiction of the Three August Ones and the Five August Emperors comes from. For in trying to make sense of the vast array of ancient founder figures, deities and beings which cluttered the mythological world of ancient China, the writers had to impose an order that reflected what they had been told to find in ancient history.

Fu Hsi, Nu Kua and Shen Nung – the Three August Ones

Out of the confusion of conflicting myths emerged certain figures who were endowed with special moral and social virtues. Fu Hsi, Nu Kua and Shen Nung arose from a melee of other deities to occupy a central role as culture bearers, as deities who brought certain vital skills and disciplines to the people and illustrated the virtuous role of wise guides. These three figures are not Emperors or rulers. They are divine or semi-divine beings who open the door to human civilization. Two of them, Fu Hsi and Nu Kua, are half human, half animal, marking in themselves the shift they were helping humans make from just one species amongst many to human civilization. Shen Nung however is purely human in form, and comes last in the classic Han dynasty (206 BC – 220 AD) chronology of the Three August Ones.

These three figures are portrayed as founder figures of the human race and especially of the Chinese. They are portrayed as ruler gods who have power over the world and who have to deal with what might be described as 'settling down' problems of the world such as collapsing skies, feuding giants, providing an explanation of where humans come from, and inventing all those things that make life liveable such as farming, weaving, music, writing and agriculture. They are also the precursors of the magical arts such as divination and astrology.

Yet the hints that remain tantalisingly buried in the texts are that this hierarchy of three supreme ordering demi-gods is a creation which does little justice to the complexity of beliefs of the early Chinese. What is still clear despite the hard work of the dynastic historians and their Confucian vision of the past, is that the original myths and traditions of early China are irredeemably shamanistic.

The Five August Rulers

After the Three August Ones come the Five August Emperors – the Yellow Emperor, Chuan Hsu, Kao Hsin, Yao and Shun. Of these, only Yao and Shun are depicted as normal human beings. The others are all gods or demi-gods who combine diverse attributes of divinity with attempting to rule the world as Emperors should do. The cycle of stories associated with the Yellow Emperor are typical of this, combining cosmic battles with evil forces, supernatural struggles, disciplining the gods and regulating the physical world. Likewise the stories of Chuan Hsu capture the extraordinary complexity of traditions which the Confucians had to either ignore, sideline or weave as adeptly as possible into the stories of the glorious past. Chuan Hsu is obviously a complex deity who does not really belong in a comfortable table of dynastic descent.

It is only when we get to Yao and Shun that the writers can begin to find a real pattern which they can work upon. Indeed, this is reflected in the old claim that time as we understand it only began with Yao.

The attempt to reduce all primal mythology to an ordered moralistic system of Confucian values was obviously well established by the time that Chuang Tzu was composed, in about 4th century BC – for in that book the author mocks the moralizing of the ancient gods. He points out that the morality doesn't always seem to fit the case – that, in other words, certain rather awkward details have survived about each of these August ones which raises questions about whether they were as they are portrayed. For the author of the Chuang Tzu, the problem with the Confucian Order and Morality version of mythology is that it goes against the Tao.

Regarding the two masters you mentioned,[Shun and Yao] what was so great about them as to be worthy of special mention? Their nit-picking philosophies make them like people who go around poking holes in walls and fences and sowing wild seeds in these places. They are like balding men contemplating combing their hair, or like a cook who counts each grain of rice before cooking! They take painstaking care, but to what end? They are useless to the world! If people of worth are elevated, there will be chaos as people fight to be promoted. If you choose people on the basis of their knowledge, then the people will try to steal this from each other. None of this makes the people any better. Indeed, what happens is that the people become more ambitious for gain. A son will kill his father for it and a minister will kill his ruler. People will steal in broad daylight and break down walls in the middle of the day. I say to you, the roots of all this great trouble will be found to have begun with Yao and Shun, and the consequences of this will remain for a thousand generations. A thousand generations later you will still have men who will eat each other!

(From Chapter 23, *The Book of Chuang Tzu*, translated by Palmer et al, Penguin, 1996)

The Tao – Returning to Ancient Roots

We need at this point to look at the fundamental cosmology which came to be imposed upon these early myths, for without understanding this it becomes increasingly difficult to understand what is going on, or perhaps even more importantly, what is not going on.

I have mentioned above that the earliest Chinese myths do not have a creation story. Indeed, the one story which appears to have a creation dimension – that of Pan Ku – is a late invention, coming into being long after the earlier accounts of Fu Hsi, Nu Kua, the Yellow Emperor and colleagues.

We have opened the Origins section with a quote from the 4th century BC text the *Tao Te Ching*, the great philosophical classic of Taoism, or more properly of China itself. In what is in effect a credal statement about origins, the *Tao Te Ching* talks thus:

The Tao
gives birth to the One;
The One
gives birth to the two;
The Two
give birth to the three –

The Three give birth to every living thing.
All things are held in yin and carry yang:
And they are held together in the ch'i of teeming energy.
(From *Tao Te Ching*, translated by Man-Ho Kwok, Martin Palmer and Jay Ramsay, Element 1993)

This brief statement captures the heart of Chinese cosmology. Central to it is that there is no Creator, no deity or divine being at the centre. Instead we have the Tao. Tao simply means at one level, The Way, or the Path, the Road. However it is used in Chinese philosophy to describe the True Way of Nature, or the Natural Way. The Tao thus becomes the innate being-ness or nature of Nature. So the Tao, what Nature is, gives rise to the One – Nature. From Nature come the twin forces which create all beings, animate and inanimate. These two forces are yin and yang.

Yin and yang are described in the texts given at the start of the Origins section. Yin is female, moist, cold, the moon, the autumn and winter, the shadow and the waters. Yang is male, dry, hot, the sun, the spring and summer, the bright and the dry land. They struggle with each other for supremacy. From their struggle comes the dynamic which drives the whole of life. For they are found locked together in every being, every situation. As one seems to be gaining the ascendancy, the other arises for they each carry the seed of the other within them as the yin yang symbol so clearly illustrates.

From the yin and yang, dynamic opposites, come the three. The three are Heaven, Earth and Humanity. These three forces are the essential elements of the universe. Heaven is another way of describing in non-theistic terms the supreme power of the being of Tao. Earth is the Tao manifest in physical form. And humanity holds the balance. Heaven is yang and Earth is yin; Heaven is round, Earth is square. Humanity holds the balance between these opposites and it is our role to ensure that when one begins to get out of control, the balance is restored.

The roots of yin and yang can be traced to the earliest clear cycles of myths: those of the struggle of Yi against the nine false suns and that of Yu against the floods. Yang – suns; yin – waters. For a people whose lands are alternatively ravaged by drought or by floods, these two forces were fundamental maverick aspects of Nature. To control them was essential. To ignore them lethal.

Whether the yin/yang philosophy gave rise to the Yi/Yu cycles or whether it was vice versa, is now almost impossible to say. I suspect they arose symbiotically.

In the Yi/Yu – Yang/Yin cycles, the necessity to order and control the primal forces is uppermost in the motifs of the myths. Woven around this are the later filial, courtly and imperial motifs of the Confucians. But I do feel that in these cycles of stories we get to hear real echoes of the earliest myths. The stories contain such strong images and incorporate so much which even the editors of the histories could not cut out, that I feel here we are closest to sampling the way in which early myths of China functioned.

The story of Pan Ku and that of the deities of Tai Shan raise further issues and questions. As I have indicated above, the Pan Ku story is much later than anything else contained within the Origins section. The story has a roundness and polish which indicates that it was written to deal with certain issues rather than emerging from oral tradition and through the cutting knife of Confucian editors. It is first recorded in the third century AD, long after the other material given in this section. We have included it because it does contain a fascinating and un-Chinese understanding of the role and significance of human beings. Whereas the other stories of the origins of human beings stress their special nature and of course their special role, the Pan Ku story claims we come from the bugs upon his body! This feature and others in this story have led academics such as Anne Birrell in her magnificent *Chinese Mythology* (The Johns Hopkins University Press, Baltimore 1993), to claim that the story originates from well outside China itself, perhaps from Central Asia or even, some have suggested, from the Near East. It is yet another example of how Chinese mythology is in fact plural.

 13

The Reclaimed Myths

The stories associated with Tai Shan fall into yet another category and offer yet another source. These are what might be called reclaimed myths. Buried in folk legends, myths and practices are traces of very ancient beliefs. At centres of religious significance, such myths and legends flow from one generation to another, absorbing or being absorbed by the newer, more powerful religious structures, but essentially surviving. Climbing the Tai Shan mountain one is swiftly aware that underneath the various layers of imperial, Buddhist and even Taoist mythology and explanation is something even older. In particular, the cult of the goddess of the mountain displays a very deep and ancient root which has been cut and trimmed by later belief systems but which essentially remains the same. Women come here, as do men after dark, to worship primal figures whose power is unrelated to Taoist, imperial or Buddhist theologies and cosmologies. By exploring these practices and the stories told by those who follow such ways it is possible to glimpse elements of older traditions and then to trace these as they twist and turn to accommodate themselves to newer ideologies. Hence the role of the goddess of Heaven, who causes nature to come to life and flow down from Tai Shan, becomes adopted into the cult of the emperors who wanted to be seen as the Sons of Heaven and therefore came to Tai Shan to commandeer the power of the Heavenly Goddess.

In dealing with such reclaimed myths one has to be very careful not to project one's own mythic needs onto the past, though to some extent this is always happening. But even given that, these reclaimed myths can offer glimpses again of older structures which have no place for the Three August Ones and the Five August Emperors, for they are remnants of very ancient tribal deities who adequately explained both where everything came from and why that particular mountain, so dominant in that tribe's social geography, could be counted as the centre of the world. As will be known to many, the Chinese name for China is Middle Country. This literally means that the Chinese saw and to some extent still see China as being in the centre of the world. This tradition traces itself back to the tribal and local myths of ancient China which saw no need to explain how everything came into being or from whence it came (except in general terms), but who did see their piece of land, their mountain, as being the centre of the universe. It is one of the features of world religions over against indigenous religions that they have to abandon any specific links to a given part of the world and have to universalize their teachings. Indigenous Chinese belief has never tried to be a world religion and remains to this day largely geographically located.

For example, one of the most famous Chinese divination books is the *Three Lives*. To this day, this book is consulted by many Chinese when a boy is born. For by using the child's horoscope, it is believed that you can find out who he was in his previous life, roughly what sort of life he will have this time round and where he will be reborn in the next life. This book, a fascinating fusion of Taoist, Buddhist and Confucian ideas and beliefs, is typical of Chinese indigenous belief. So it comes as no surprise to discover that in looking at past lives or at future lives, the authors could only conceive of those taking place in given parts of China. According to this book, all lives have been lived, are lived and will be lived within the provinces of China. No mention is made anywhere of any other country.

Shamanic Influences

It is perhaps worth turning now to look at the religious and cultural background from which the earliest myths came. I have briefly mentioned above that shamanism lies behind and within the fragments of the early myths. But what was shamanism and why were the Confucian historians so anxious to expunge it from the records?

Shamanism can lay claim to being the oldest world religion, though it is unlike anything that we would consider a world religion today. It seems to have first appeared in the wastes of Siberia. From there, ten thousand years ago at least, it spread out into Mongolia and China and on further south; east across the land bridge which then linked Siberia with Alaska, into North and central America; west across the tundra to reach the shores of Finland. All this took thousands of years. None of it was directed by anything except migration patterns and the appeal of a religious system which acknowledged the power of nature but also sought to influence it towards the wellbeing of humans.

Shamanism posits two worlds of existence. The first and most important and real one is the spiritual world. The second world is our world of physical reality. The two lie side by side and occasionally break in upon each other. By entering into a trance, the shaman is able to communicate with the spirit world. Or to be more precise, is able to be taken over by elements of the spirit world who thus can communicate with this world. As illness, fate and fortune are shaped by the spirit world, communication is vital. The shaman opens a two-way means of interaction between the worlds of spirit and physical. But he or she can also open communication between the human world and the animal world. This is why shamans are usually depicted or described as being half animal, half human. The most common forms of animal manifestation are the bear or the stag. Some of the most ancient rock paintings in France and in Central Asia depict dancers wearing deerskins and antlers, while the painted cave sequence found in France in late 1994 seems to have evidence of worship of a bear skull. All this dates back to possibly 25,000 years ago. In dealing with shamanism we are dealing with the earliest traceable religious instinct of humanity.

In China shamanism appears to have been the main formal expression of religion for millennia. From the earliest written records of China we find shamanism central to life. Indeed the earliest written records were compiled by shamans who had evolved a complex series of divinational processes, thus regularizing and controlling contact between the two worlds. The shamans used tortoise shells or ox bones to seek answers to specific questions from the spirits of the other world. The answers manifested themselves in cracks on the shells or bones as the result of applying heated sticks to certain spots. These cracks were then read by the shaman priests and if the oracle they gave proved to be an important one, the answer was inscribed upon the shell or bone more clearly and kept as a record. Hundreds of thousands of these oracle bones have been found dating back to around 1700 BC at the earliest and continuing up into the Chou dynasty – until around 900 BC.

One of the key sources of mythology mentioned earlier are the Songs of the South. These are shamanistic songs capturing the world view of late shamanism – around 400 BC. By this time sham-anism had become unfashionable in the Confucian controlled northern areas of China. The Songs of the South come from the Chou kingdom and represent the final fling of a tradition which was about to be overwhelmed by the more rational rising power of the Chin who were to become the first to unite all China physically.

But the process of reducing the power of the shamans had been going on for some time. Under the Shang dynasty (around

1750 – 1122 BC) they held immense power, almost on a par with the ruler. They inspired the Chou tribes to invade in the 12th century BC, but within a short period of time they were being marginalized. It is almost as if their primal roots and links with the rugged mountains and beliefs of their former tribal selves were an embarrassment to the Chou.

The real death knell came with the rise of Confucian values with their emphasis on the urban and urbane society with its clear hierarchies and power-lines, which ignored or at the most simply sidelined the issue of the otherworld. When it became important to create a Confucian version of early history, the great shaman figures such as Fu Hsi, Nu Kua, Kun, Yu and so forth were cleansed of their shamanistic associations and turned into moral exemplars.

By the mid Han period, around 50 BC, the shamans had been almost totally marginalized in both history and in contemporary society. They were to re-emerge again in a new guise some two hundred years later in popular Taoism. But they never reclaimed the lost myths which were preserved in the official records of the great historians.

It is interesting that one of the few places where the shamans are allowed to appear in the purged records and accounts is in relation to the story of Kun. When the failed, flawed hero Kun dies, it is shamans who keep watch upon his body until after three years it splits and forth comes the real hero Yu, whereupon Kun is transformed into a giant yellow bear. Here is a hero who could not do what was requested, who cheated, who deceived and who lost. In this context the shamanic link is not denied.

Confucian Myths

While we have to hunt, scratch, search and reclaim the most ancient myths, this is not the case when we come to the other main categories of myths which we offer in this book. For each of the others, Confucian, Taoist, Buddhist and folk, we have lineages which have remained unbroken, even if the myths have changed from time to time in their emphasis, or been remoulded to take account of new ideas.

In the Confucian myths we meet a problem of terminology. Kung Fu Tzu is famous for his response to questions about the divine, the spiritual and the otherworld. He basically said he had enough trouble sorting out, dealing with and understanding this world without trying to take on the world of the spirits. It is perhaps one of the more subtle ironies of history that Kung Fu Tzu, the rationalist and moralist, should end up being worshipped as a god. Yet despite a long tradition of deifying humans – of which more later – Kung Fu Tzu has not gathered around him mythic elements in the way that virtually all other humans-become-gods have in China. In part this is because the records of his life are fairly full and were kept by a living lineage of scholars who were quick to scotch any attempts to enhance them with supernatural dimensions. In part it was because Kung Fu Tzu's significance was mainly this worldly in terms of shaping and guiding imperial bureaucracy and life.

There is a whole corpus of stories which can be classified as Confucian. These are often depicted on the walls of Confucian temples or even in other temples. They are the twenty six stories of exemplary filial piety. These moral, and often tedious, tales espouse such values as respect for grandparents; respect from the daughter in law to the father or mother in law; respect for the emperor and so forth. Stories of exemplary filial piety were woven into the reading books of children and young scholars. For example, under the precept 'Honour your mother and father' readers would find the story of Huang Hsiang, who from the age of nine knew how to warm his parents' bed so that they could retire to bed in comfort. Or there is the tale of the grand-daughter in law who feeds the toothless grandfather with milk from her own breast, even at the expense of her baby in order to provide the old man with nourishment.

A classic of the Confucian story is that of Su Wu who despite terrible sufferings, never relinquishes his virtuous stand of being faithful to his Emperor. This is set off in classic narrative style by the betrayal of such loyalty by his companion Li Ling.

The end result is that while there are many stories about those who acted in accordance with Confucian rules, none of these could be classified as a myth in conventional language.

But we have included a couple of Confucian moral tales because they are important to lay alongside the usual supernatural tales of the Buddhists and Taoists and in order to see what forces had shaped the ancient myths into attempts at morality stories.

Confucianism meets Taoism

While Confucian stories show how Heaven rewards those who follow the Tao of filial piety, we should perhaps look at one story which we have put under the Taoism section. The story of Kuan Ti.

Here is a moral tale. A heroic fighter pledges his honour to the dying Han dynasty. Through trials and tribulations he remains faithful to this pledge. He defends the honour of those in authority over him and protects the weak and the defenceless. As such he embodies many of the virtues of a good Confucian. Indeed, it seems to have been these attributes which led to his promotion by various emperors, from being just a heroic human to being described as Faithful and Loyal Deity, Supporter of Heaven and Protector of the Realm in 1594.

While Kuan Ti embodies all these Confucian, imperial values, it is as the God who protects against evil forces that he is most popular in folk religion. The story of the actors illustrates the shift from Confucian moral hero to supernatural fighter against evil spirits. Because Kuan Ti is worshipped for his supernatural powers more than for his moral example, we have included his story in the Taoist section. Yet in a very real way he emerges because of Confucian values and it is for these that he is celebrated in the famous novel based upon his life and times, called *The Romance of the Three Kingdoms*. This novel, written in the 14th century AD, walks a fascinating line between Confucian orthodoxy and popular religious belief. For example, the main villains in the novel (in terms of their being rebels against the legitimate dynasty) are the Yellow Turbans. These were Taoist rebels who are depicted in the book as using magic and occult powers, forces which the heroes also have to resort to at times when fighting against them.

While the emphasis in the novel is on the struggle between Confucian values of order, authority and obedience to those above, it nevertheless leaves space for supernatural incidents and forces.

And here lies the main feature of the backdrop to Chinese mythologies: the fact that all traditions overlap and are used by the people of China as and when it is convenient to do so. This needs to be held in mind as we explore deeper into the major clusters such as Taoist or Buddhist. For most Chinese there is no significant difference in meaning or use between these different groups. People will quite happily worship deities from both traditions, side by side.

Taoist myths

I want to now turn to the mythological world of Taoism and to an exploration of Taoism itself.

Taoism takes its name from the word 'Tao' which we explored above. As a popular religion it originates in the second century AD but its roots are older than that. At one level it was the old shamanism given new and more socially acceptable form. Much of the magic, the trances, the reception of messages from the other spirit world, owes its origin to shamanism. But it was also heir to the anti-Confucian, anti-establishmentarian traditions of writers such as Chuang Tzu and Lieh Tzu. We have already seen that Chuang Tzu mocked the sanitized mythology of the Confucians. From this tradition came the rejection of reliance upon human reasoning as a way to understanding. From the Tao Te Ching came the notion of *wu wei* – of action through non-action; of going with the flow and thus being able to achieve by being part of that which is.

The flavour of Taoist mythology is anti-establishment, pro the poor and highly supernatural. Gods, goddesses, demons, spirits, ghosts and humans possessed of extraordinary magical powers flow in and out of Taoist tales. These deities are not the clear cut good or bad deities of Buddhist mythology, but reflect the more primal energy of ambiguity, of a time when human relationship with the gods and goddesses was one of ambivalence and uncertainty. It reflects the shamanistic view of the spiritual as more powerful but not necessarily more moral. For example this lovely story captures something of the ambiguity of the Taoist relationship with and understanding of the supernatural world.

A group of students had gathered at a spirit writing altar in order to ask for a message about their future prospects. The spirit wrote

'Drunkard Chao has come.' The students were furious saying, 'We requested Immortal Lu. What is a crude ghost doing interfering! We shall ask the Immortal to use his sword to execute you.'

The spirit stopped writing for a while then started again. 'The Taoist Immortal Lu Tung Pin happened to be passing. What do you want to ask?'

The students solemnly bowed twice and then enquired how they would each fare in the forthcoming exams. The spirit wrote, 'Prepare more ink.' So the students took their ink sticks and prepared more ink which they each poured into a bowl. Kneeling, they asked what they should do next. The spirit wrote, 'Share the ink between you and drink it, then I shall tell you what is going to happen.'

The students shared out the ink and drank it. When they had finished, the spirit wrote in large letters, 'Normally you don't study; now you drink ink at the last moment. I am not the Immortal Lu; I am still the Drunkard Chao!'

Hearing this the students were enraged and smashed up the altar.

(Adapted from the translation of Wu Chi Chang's story given on page 11 of A *God's Own Tale* by Terry F. Kleeman, State University of New York Press, 1994)

The main followers of popular Taoism were and are the ordinary peasants and workers of China, especially of South China where shamanism was able to hold sway much longer than in the north. These people's lives are ones of unremitting hardship, grind and poverty. They are at the bottom of the ladder in all aspects of Chinese life. Therefore their experience of the world was one of capriciousness and of bondage. This is reflected in what the myths offered. They offer, as in the persons of the Eight Immortals, those who would defend the poor and downtrodden; those who would reward the virtuous and punish the rich and arrogant. They offer promises of untold wealth or happiness for those who do what is right against those who exploit and usurp power.

But alongside this they also offer an accessible and manageable spirit world, albeit with capricious gods, but nevertheless with some sort of structure. They provide gods who will defend you or ways and means to influence the divine world to the extent that you can. The story of Kuan Ti illustrates the need for defender gods who will fight for you against the evil of frightening aspects of the spirit world. But at the same time, through a Heavenly bureaucracy, they also make the spirit world comprehensible.

For example, one of my Chinese colleagues is an exorcist. He is able to deal with ghosts who disturb the lives of his clients. When investigating a case, he will ask for a full description of the appearance and/or activities of the ghost or evil spirit. Once he has found out what sort of evil spirit it is he can classify it. There is a clear scale of ghosts and evil spirits and each has its opponent, and its appropriate charm, from the Taoist folk religious pantheon. Having identified what kind of ghost it is, he can call up the attacking deity, invoke the defending constellation and write the appropriate charm which once burnt will cleanse the area of this particular malignant force.

When the spirit world is so organized, it is possible to feel you have got a grip on life when your normal circumstances might tell you otherwise.

But at the heart of the Taoist vision is the credal statement from chapter 42 of the Tao Te Ching which was quoted earlier and is given at the start of the Origin section. For fundamental to Taoism is a belief that humanity is here to balance out the universe – to be the third element of the triad of Heaven, Earth and Humanity. Through its rich tradition of liturgies it offers a unifying and stabilizing vision of the place of humanity in the overall purpose of the Tao. But it also stresses that the main role humans can play is to go with the flow and not to try to master nature and force it to go against its innate nature, for that way lies disaster.

The Pursuit of Immortality

Taoism also holds that human beings can achieve immortality but only through preservation of this physical body. The pursuit of immortality is one of two strands of Taoism identified by the China Taoist Association when they presented to the outside world the core teachings of Taoism. In their General Statement on Taoism published as a preamble to the Taoist Declaration on Nature in 1995, they wrote the following:

1. Give respect to the Tao above everything else.

Tao simply means 'the way'. Taoism considers that the Tao is the origin of everything, and Tao is the ultimate aim of all Taoists. This is the fundamental tenet of Taoism. Tao is the way of Heaven, Earth and Humanity. The Tao took form in the being of the Grandmother Goddess. She came to Earth to enlighten humanity. She taught the people to let everything grow according to its own course without interference. This is called the way of no-action, no-selfishness (wu-wei), and this principle is an important rule for Taoists. It teaches them to be very plain and modest, and not to struggle with others for personal gain in their material life. This kind of virtue is the ideal spiritual kingdom for which the followers of Taoism long.

2. Give great value to life.

Taoism pursues immortality. It regards life as the most valuable thing. Master Chang Tao Ling (c 2nd century AD) said that life is another expression of Tao, and the study of Tao includes the study of how to extend one's life. With this principle in mind, many Taoists have undertaken considerable exploration in this regard. They believe that life is not controlled by Heaven, but by

human beings themselves. People can prolong life through meditation and exercise. The exercises include both the moral and
the physical sides. People should train their will, discard selfish-
ness and the pursuit of fame, do good deeds and seek to become
a model of virtue (te).

(Quoted from *Taoism – Ecology and Faith*, published by WWF UK,
1995)

This basic outline of contemporary Taoism's self understanding is
fascinating for our study of mythology for a number of reasons. We
have already looked at Tao and its meaning for Taoists. We have
also encountered the Grandmother Goddess for she is the founder
goddess who is still worshipped at Tai Shan and who is referred to
in the story about Tai Shan in Origins. Here we see a pre-formal
Taoism deity being integrated into a later philosophy, but with
many of her primal powers and significance still intact.

The anti-material, worldly success ethos of the Immortals is
also set out. This emphasis in Taoism is well captured in The
Immortal's Dream where the aspiring and successful bureaucrat
Lu Tung Pin is given a vision of the purposelessness of such success, and thus enlightened gives it all up to study to become an
immortal.

In section 2 of the above extract, the crucial statement about
one's life being one's own, not Heaven's, is given. This is important because Taoism is not fatalistic. It offers the poor and the
hopeless the possibility that through their own actions their lives
could be changed and transformed.

A fine example of that is given in the story of the woman who
put straw in the feng shui master's water. Through her act of
thoughtful kindness, even though it was not understood by the
master, she earned Heaven's blessing. And that was despite the
feng shui master giving her advice which should have brought
death and disaster upon her and her family!

The Taoist Pantheon

The world of the deities of Taoism is vast, complex and largely redundant in that usually only a score or so of deities actually hold key significance to Taoist or folk religion believers. The following attempts to put in a few words the core aspects of that world in order that the stories given can be placed within their background. As I have stressed above, we have sought to choose myths and legends which capture something of the fundamental values which Taoism expresses, and we have not tried to present a full pantheon of the gods for in many cases the stories associated with them stress their bureaucratic function rather than offer us any deeper insight into the world view of Taoism itself.

At the head of the Taoist pantheon are the Past, Present and Future Emperors of Heaven. The first, The Primal Heaven Honoured One, ruled in the distant past, from the time when yin and yang first came to be until the beginnings of recorded history. The Emperor of the present is the Heaven Honoured Jade Emperor. Jade is seen as the embodiment of the yang principle and thus as the ultimate masculine symbol of perfection. The Jade Emperor rules all Heaven today and oversees the world below. He is mocked in many of the Monkey stories (*see pages* 159–195) where his inability to control Monkey brings derision upon his head and it is only when the Buddha intervenes that the Jade Emperor is saved from the actions of Monkey.

The final Emperor of Heaven is the future ruler known as the Heaven Honoured One of the Coming of the Jade of the Golden Gate.

It is quite clear from this structure that Taoism here is imitating Buddhism with its Buddha of the Past, Buddha of the Present and Future Buddha. For the Jade Emperor seems to have only emerged around the year 1007 when a mere mortal emperor was losing power and authority until the Jade Emperor came and 'revealed' to him that he was blessed by Heaven.

It has to be said that while the Jade Emperor rules Heaven at the top of the pantheon, he has two rivals who seem as popular. Lao Tzu, the almost certainly mythic founder of Taoism and author of the Tao Te Ching, is revered by Taoist thinkers as the real ultimate being in Heaven, and is often seen as the physical embodiment of the Tao itself. But another immensely powerful and popular figure is the Queen Mother of the West. As the Jade Emperor is supreme yang, the Queen Mother of the West is ultimate yin. Her title direction, West, is the direction of the dying sun, the decline of yin. It is also the direction of death. She presides over the fate of those who wish to achieve immortality, offering the possibility of feasting with her in her palace on the Peaches of Immortality. She is a powerful rather than benevolent figure and brings a primal energy to the rather eviscerate Court of the Jade Emperor.

And so she should for she is a pre-Taoist deity who has managed not only to survive into the new dispensation but even enhance her role.

Mention of a Queen Mother of the West goes back to the fifth or fourth century BC. Hints of her can be found in the Tao Te Ching and she is explicitly mentioned by Chuang Tzu who interestingly records that no one knows of her beginning or origin. She was obviously, even then, c350 BC, a mysterious primal figure.

Her cult grew rapidly in the early Han period (c210 – 6 BC) until she became the centre of apocalyptic cults around 6 BC, in which oppressed peasants arose against their masters, only to be put down swiftly. This hardly endeared her to Confucian historians and commentators, but despite their disapproval, her cult continued to grow, albeit in less violent ways.

When Taoism appeared as a coherent religious system, the Queen Mother of the West became one of its major deities, revealing scriptures which formed the basis of one of the major schools of Taoism. Her integration into Taoism as a religious system ensured her survival and the continuity of her following. She remains a strange, remote figure – not one to trifle with. Her appearance in later versions of stories, such as the story of Yi the Archer's quest for immortality (*see page* 55) or in the Monkey stories (*see pages* 59–195) of the 16th century, show a more amenable side of her. However, in popular devotion, the primal and pre-historic elements of her not only survive but continue to define her role and power.

Under the Jade Emperor and the Queen Mother of the West comes a vast array of officials each with their own ministry. In the story of Wen Chang, the god of Literature, we see one such official at work. Kuan Ti as God of War is another. There are hundreds of figures like them – ministers of Thunder, Water, Fire, Medicine, Smallpox, of the Ten Courts of Hell. Under them come regional gods. Every province of China has its guardian deity, every city, every town. Within towns or cities there are gods for each district; for each street; for each house. All are ranked in accordance with their significance. Within the house there is a god of the kitchen, a god of the bathroom and so on.

The role of these gods is very similar to that of their more earthly counterparts: namely to keep a watch over the world or their bit of it and to report anything going on or wrong within it.

What is perhaps most surprising with regard to these deities is that most of them began life as ordinary human beings. Their progression to deity is a mixture of the quality of their own lives or the strengths of their personalities and powers, combined with popular interest and sometimes official, even imperial, sanction. For example, the God of old Peking city was an official called Yang Ki Sheng who was executed in 1556 aged forty but who had been falsely accused. By popular acclaim he was elected as the City god, replacing an older one who simply had not been up to the mark.

One of the most famous of these city gods was Yue Fei. For many centuries he was the city god of Hangchow. His story is a good example of how a local hero becomes a deity. His story is included in the Confucian section for he exemplifies the true virtues of a Confucian. Yet it is both as such a model and as the deified popularly acclaimed city god of Hangchow that he is remembered today. His temple and tomb can be visited to this day.

Evil Spirits and Demons

Against this Heavenly pantheon of responsible deities are ranked the masses of evil spirits and demons. Most of these are restless human spirits who have been unable to be reborn or take up their honoured position as ancestors because of some terrible crime they committed or because they have no descendants to offer funeral goods and prayers for their wellbeing. Other spirits are agents of the various ministries, especially those of Hell, who have a punishment or moral function.

In a world where every year has its own deity, each day is watched over by good and bad spirits and when every hour has its good luck or bad luck influence, the physical world is wrapped up and encapsulated in the spiritual world. What remains consistent is that the old shamanistic understanding that the spirit world is more powerful, even more real than this physical one, remains. Life has to be undertaken by negotiating your way through with the aid of the gods.

Perhaps the most distinguishing feature of Taoist mythology is the interventionist element of figures such as the Immortals who will suddenly decide to act. Believing in the Taoist deities is a little like playing the lottery. You just never know when you might be blessed!

Buddhism

It is perhaps significant that in discussing Buddhism and Chinese mythology, one is looking as much at what China gave to Buddhism as to what Buddhism gave to China

Of the three great faiths of China, Buddhism is the foreign import and has had to struggle under that image for all of its nearly two thousand years in China. What has happened to the Buddhism which entered China sometime in the first century AD is that it has been taken over and redeveloped by the Chinese in distinctive ways. Not least of these have been the reworkings of Buddhism to provide a vehicle for mythological and epic tales on a par with that of the native faith of Taoism. Indeed, for many people it is impossible to tell the two traditions apart at the mythological level.

The traditional story of the introduction of Buddhism to China is itself a myth. It is said that around the year 65 AD, the Han dynasty emperor Ming (58 – 75 AD) had a dream. In his dream he saw a golden man flying before him as he watched from his palace. The next day he enquired of his advisers what this dream might signify. One minister, Fu Yi, said that he had heard of a wise one in India who had achieved salvation and was known as the Buddha. He said the Buddha was able to fly and was of a golden colour. The Emperor concluded that the Buddha had personally appeared to him and that he must find out more about the Golden Man of the West.

The Emperor despatched envoys to India to find out more of this Golden Man and to bring back any teachings and books which could explain this faith. The envoys travelled to Afghanistan, then a centre of Buddhism under the influence of the Greek states founded by Alexander the Great. Here the envoys are reputed to have found two monks willing to return to China with them, and to bring Buddhist sutras to translate.

When the envoys returned triumphantly to the capital, Luoyang, they brought the sutras on the back of a white horse. To this day it is possible to visit what claims to be the first Buddhist temple in China, near Luoyang and it is still called the White Horse Temple. The two monks from Afghanistan lie buried in the temple precincts.

Many reject the story of Emperor Ming's dream out of hand, whilst acknowledging that Buddhism first began to penetrate in a serious way during the first century AD. I feel the story wonderfully captures the mixture of fable and fact that makes Chinese Buddhist mythology so classically Chinese. For it falls into exactly the pattern we have seen in Taoism – namely, the taking of an historical incident or person and the mythologizing of that in order to create a better story for didactic or even straight entertainment purposes.

The interaction between Taoism and Buddhism is a specialist field of its own and not one we can look at in any detail here. I have already noted the influence of Buddhism on the concept of the Supreme Three in Taoism. Likewise there is interaction between Taoism and Buddhism on the gruesome details of Hell. In Taoism there are ten hells, ruled over by judges and each one ascribed a different function or to deal with diverse sins. In Buddhism there are eighteen hells. In the tales and legends that surround these multitudinous hells, common themes and images are to be found aplenty between the two faiths and there is little doubt that the notion of hells, introduced almost certainly by Buddhism, drew upon Taoist exorcism imagery and together created one of the nastiest sets of religious horror stories ever invented.

One of the most successful means of spreading the Buddhist faith used in China throughout its earliest period, and influential to this day in improving stories, are the pien-wen stories. These are wonderfully colourful elaborations upon a Buddhist theme, sometimes taking an incident from the sutras or a text and building an entire story around them. One of the most famous is that told of Mu Lien. In the telling of a story about the arhat Mu Lien, the Buddhists of China tackled head on one of the charges levelled against them by the Confucians: namely, that becoming a monk or nun was to act in an unfilial way – to abandon one's responsibilities for one's parents. This charge, frequently levelled against Buddhism in China, was a major stumbling block in the attempt by Buddhism to become socially acceptable in China.

Mu Lien had through countless lives achieved arhatship – nirvana – by his own efforts. Having achieved nirvana, he wished to bestow upon his parents his blessing. Using his divine powers, he scanned the three worlds to find out where they had been reincarnated.

To his distress he found his mother had been reborn as a hungry ghost, haunting the world looking for food to be offered to her by those who cared for the wicked souls who were thus reborn. Mu Lien, moved by compassion and filial sorrow, immediately brought her a bowl of food. But no sooner did she lift it to her lips than it became burning coals. In deep distress Mu Lien journeyed to see the Buddha to enquire the reason for this.

To his horror he heard from the Buddha that the crimes his mother had committed were so grievous that nothing Mu Lien could do would change her fortune, even though as an arhat he had such virtue. Mu Lien was stunned to hear this but his love for his mother was so great that he pressed the Buddha as to whether there was anything anyone could do to help her.

The Buddha replied that there was only one way she could be helped. If all the monks of the ten quarters were brought together at one time, they could through their combined powers and goodness release her from her sufferings as a hungry ghost.

Mu Lien vowed that he was willing to try such a feat. To this the Buddha replied that he should prepare a vast and wonderful banquet and summon all the monks of the ten quarters to join him on the fifteenth day of the seventh moon. This invitation, the

Buddha commanded, should be made in the name of parents of the last seven generations. If all the monks accepted this invitation and partook of the banquet, then it would be possible for Mu Lien's mother to escape her present fate. The beneficial effects of such a banquet would affect all those who were in torment, back seven generations and would bring blessings upon parents alive today.

Mu Lien did as he had been commanded. On the fifteenth day of the seventh moon, monks streamed in from the ten quarters. All came, none stayed away. The banquet was a great success and as a result Mu Lien's mother was released from her existence as a hungry ghost and reborn as a human again.

Mu Lien returned in gratitude to the Buddha and asked for one last boon. 'Is it possible for those sons who are filial and devout to offer such a feast regularly to ensure the well being of their parents and of saving their ancestors from the horrors of terrible reincarnations?'

The Buddha replied 'Indeed it is and to be welcomed. Let all such filial and devout sons hold such a festival on the fifteenth day of the seventh moon. Those disciples of the Buddha who are filial and obedient to their parents must constantly remember their parents and make offerings for them and for the seven generations.'

In pien-wen stories such as this Buddhism tackled difficult questions and created, quite consciously, a mythology which gave meaning to its actions, festivals and core beliefs. What is clear in Chinese Buddhism is that at times Buddhism set out to tackle issues by the creation of new myths. Whether this was always as consciously done as in the case of many of the pien-wen is a matter of debate, but a very clear example of this is to be found in the story of Miao-shan or Kuan Yin as she is revealed to be.

The Miao-shan story is one of the best recorded in Chinese literature for we know, to the very day, when the story was first publicly promoted, and we can even see why. What is extraordinary about the story is that it drew to it many other legends and myths and fashioned a new goddess out of them. In a way, it is a very long pien-wen – for at the heart of the Kuan Yin story lies a canonical Buddhist text which briefly describes the virtues and attributes of a bodhisattva. From this grew an entire mythology which not only changed the sex of the bodhisattva from male to female, but brought in fantastical dimensions which are entirely Chinese in nature.

The goddess Kuan Yin arises from the Chinese translation of the name of the bodhisattva Avalokitesvara from the Lotus Sutra. Avalokitesvara is described as being compassionate and able to manifest himself in many different forms in order to reach out to and help countless people from diverse backgrounds. It was this transforming and interactive aspect which swiftly made Avalokitesvara/Kuan Yin one of the most popular Buddhist deities during the Tang dynasty (618 – 907 AD). For reasons too complex to enter into here (but see *Kuan Yin* by Martin Palmer, Jay Ramsay with Kwok Man Ho, Thorsons, 1995) Kuan Yin became a female deity and drew to her over the centuries many other myths and legends associated with goddesses in ancient China – especially those associated with sea goddesses. But the core myth is the one told in this book, the story of Miao Shan.

In the year 1100, a local official paid a visit to a monastery in the hills of Honan, where a Kuan Yin temple already existed. While visiting he was told of a remarkable book which had been given to the monastery by a mysterious visitor only a few weeks earlier. This book claimed to tell of the incarnation of Kuan Yin in the form of a woman, Miao Shan, and claimed that the very site upon which the monastery was built was where she had made herself known to her parents, as the goddess Kuan Yin.

The official erected an inscription and put immense effort into promoting the site as a major pilgrimage centre. He was very successful and the monastery at Hsiang Shan soon became very wealthy from the proceeds – which was almost certainly the intention of the abbot in passing on this book to his wealthy and influential visitor. The account of Miao Shan which was 'revealed' in

1100 is substantially that told in this book. However, over the year extra details have been added to embellish the story even further. We have included these so as to give a feel for the full story as it is told today.

Here is a detail from the Buddhist scriptures, given a new shape by the interaction with China in that the male bodhisattva becomes female, to which is then fused a major new myth which then develops its own life, draws in other, older myths and helps further the cult of the goddess. An organic myth, just as the myth of Kuan Ti is organic, and quintessentially Chinese.

It is however the stories of Monkey which offer one of the most fascinating and revealing insights into Buddhist mythology in China, indeed, offer more than that. For the story of how Monkey and his associates rose to be gods in their own right, and powerful ones at that in contemporary Chinese religion, illustrates wonderfully the dynamic and creative nature of Chinese mythology.

The origin of the Monkey stories lies in a historical event, the actual journey to India to collect Buddhist scriptures, undertaken by the Tang dynasty monk Hsuan Tsang, who in 629 set out for India. His journey is recorded in his own account called *Record of the Western Regions* and in the writings of those who knew him and offer good historical accounts of the state of Buddhism in India at the time of his travels. There is little which is supernatural or fantastical about these accounts, other than elements of classic Buddhist divine cosmology.

By the end of the tenth century, this epic journey, long a favourite subject for storytellers, is being endowed with many supernatural and fantastical features. By the 13th century, the journey of the monk, now usually called Sanzang or Tripitaka, has become a standard part of the theatrical performances at religious fairs. With Sanzang or Tripitaka are now various assistants who in differing ways represent aspects of human behaviour or types of humans. Indeed, Sanzang or Tripitaka himself has come to be a sort of Everyman, trying to make his way and make sense of his way through life. The assistants are a mixture of comic and tragic figures who exemplify human difficulties and joys. It is fast becoming what one commentator has called the Chinese Pilgrim's Progress – only funnier!

But it is with the writing of the novel Monkey by Wu Cheng En, sometime in the mid-sixteenth century, that the story really takes off. The three stories given in this book come from Wu Cheng En's mammoth work and represent just a few aspects of the vast and delightful array of stories to be found within that tome.

The novel by Wu Cheng En took hold of diverse aspects of popular tradition and historical fact and wove a seamless narrative which both promoted Buddhism, mocked Taoism, defined Confucianism as dull and elevated the prankster, the con-man and the idiot to positions of salvationary significance. In doing so, Wu tapped into a deep root of Chinese religious belief and probably did more to popularize Buddhism to the literate masses than any other person. For to this day, it is the figures of Monkey the prankster, Pigsy the fat fool and Sandy the faithful which most inform and entertain the masses of ordinary believers. In temples throughout China, both Buddhist and Taoist or folk religion, you can find episodes from the story carved, or statues of Monkey or Pigsy or Tripitaka venerated. Rarely in history has a written novel, as far as we can see as just a good read, managed to create so many new deities.

The story of the mythologizing of the historical journey of Hsuan Tsang and the deifying of the characters in the novel of Wu Cheng En illustrates more clearly than anything else the dynamic processes involved in Chinese mythology. For this is a culture where not only do historical individuals rise to become gods through imperial order, but characters from stories or novels are elevated by popular demand and belief.

Folk Religion

This brings us to the last classification and one fraught with problems. The fact of the matter is that the vast majority of Chinese people worship or make use of Buddhist and Taoist deities – and indeed anything else which comes along – indiscriminately. For example, on the pilgrimage routes to the top of great Buddhist sacred mountains such as E Mei Shan or Taoist ones such as Tai Shan, you can buy amulets of either faith at each, along with crucifixes, Islamic Hands of Fatima and other religious insignia from Muslim and Christian faiths. In everyday life, elements that can be traced back to the earliest days of shamanism rub shoulders with deities who have only emerged as significant in the last hundred years. For example, in Hong Kong worship of the local earth god, usually in the form of a small incense shrine before the front door, a practice which dates back to earliest beliefs about the spirits inhabiting the land, will be practised in a house which also hosts a statue of Wong Tai Sin, a Taoist folk deity of divination who has emerged into prominence in the last sixty or seventy years. The same house will also almost certainly have a statue of Kuan Yin to protect the children. And at the back of the main room will be the ancestor tablets, illuminated by a glowing red light – Confucian filial piety fused with earlier threads of ancestor worship.

To the ordinary Chinese, attempting to make sense of life, all and any supernatural forces are welcome if they help! A Taoist temple in a market place might have The Queen Mother of the West at its heart, with a side room filled with the sixty different year gods of the Chinese calendrical cycle of sixty years. In another shrine will be Kuan Yin and beside her Monkey, Pigsy and Tripitaka. The local fortune teller will use Buddhist, Taoist and indefinable systems of divination, calling equally upon the divinatory powers of the I Ching – shamanistic in origin; the Jade Emperor's Fortune poems – Taoist; Maitraya Buddha's forecasts – Buddhist; and possibly a local deity who belongs to no one definable tradition.

It is this milieu, this mixing pot, which forms the crucible of Chinese mythology and which keeps the mythology alive to this day.

I began by claiming that there is no one Chinese mythology, but mythologies. To travel in China today is to discover the truth of this at every step. Local legends, local versions of great mythic themes, local versions of deities abound. And Communism has done little to change this. All it has added are new sources of myths – to do with the miraculous preservation of statues during the destructive times of the Cultural Revolution or the wonderful manifestations of deities during times of intense trouble. Even under the worst times of Communist control, the myths were not abolished or ignored but reworked. The Monkey story – up to the point of him challenging Heaven – was used to extol the virtues of plebeian rebellion against the forces of ancient feudal power; the story of Yue Fei was reworked to encourage patriotism for the People's Republic of China. The perennial Taoist theme of resistance to bureaucracy and the powerful by the downtrodden was fully appreciated by Communist ideologists and they even developed their own versions of key mythological themes.

At their core, Chinese mythologies explore remarkably similar terrain. The fear cum control of natural forces such as disease or floods. They provide a sense of belonging, a feeling of knowing your place and being secure within it in an apparently chaotic cosmos. The provision of supernatural allies in the struggle against stronger foes, both natural – human – and supernatural – demons. The promise of reward for justice and integrity no matter how hard the path to that reward. A sense of continuity with an idealized past which shaped the present. The possible intervention of gods and goddesses at times of hardship or oppression – the list can go on. Each of the mythologies responds to essentially the same concerns and does so in remarkably similar ways. A mixture of history fused with mythology; actual individuals paired with legendary figures; the human in combination with the animal. It is the sanctification of the ordinary and the deification of the mundane which allows for all life to be purposeful and for the deities to be useful. It is the elevation of the human to divine status and the integration of the divine with the human, thus imbuing everything, no matter how minor, with eternal significance.

These themes have shaped all the mythologies of China for thousands of years and continue to do so to this very day.

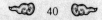

1
Origins

Tao – the Origin

The Tao
gives birth to the One:
The One
gives birth to the two;
The Two
give birth to the three –
The Three give birth to every living thing.
All things are held in yin and carry yang:
And they are held together in the ch'i of teeming energy.

Before there was that which is, when all that is was united in sameness in the emptiness of vastness. When all was empty and one, one and empty, resting without ceasing, that of the wet and that of the undefined, there was neither dark nor light.

From its home in nothing, from its place in emptiness came Tao. Tao gave rise to cosmic oneness and the cosmic oneness gave birth to Original Breath, ch'i, limited yet universal. That which was light arose and became yang, Heaven and hot and dry. That which was heavy sank and became yin, Earth and moisture and cold. The double essence of heaven and earth became yin and yang. From the interaction of yin and yang came the cycle of rise and fall, of yin rising to a peak only to fall to yang ascending, which likewise at its peak gives way to yin again, endlessly. The four seasons sprang from yin and yang, from the peak of yang in summer through the decline of yang in autumn and the rise of yin, through the peak of yin at wintertime until the ascension of yang again during spring, all is driven by the dynamic of yin and yang.

From the four seasons come the myriad beings, all of life. From the hot ch'i of yang came fire and its essence formed the sun. From the ch'i of yin came water and its essence formed the moon.

Of their nature, Heaven is round and the Earth is square.

P'an Ku – Carver of Creation

P'an Ku born at the moment of the separation of yin and yang. As Heaven formed and earth solidified, P'an Ku grew to fill the space between them. For eighteen thousand years Heaven and Earth took form and P'an Ku grew. Labouring, he took and moulded the very elements of nature. Working as the original Third in the Triad of Heaven, Earth and Humanity, he balanced yin and harmonized yang. With his hammer and chisel he fashioned the fabric of the world until, worn out by his labours and his great antiquity, he collapsed and died.

And it was then, some say, that life upon the earth began. His breath became the wind and clouds and his voice that of thunder. His arms and legs and the five extremities became the four points of the compass and the five sacred mountains. His blood and semen became rivers and lakes. His muscles and veins formed the arteries of the earth while his flesh became the rich soil of the ground. His hair became the trees and plants and his teeth and bones formed metal ores and rocks while from his marrow came jewels of great value. His sweat became the pouring rain. And from the bugs upon his body, so some say, came the peoples of the world.

Fu Hsi and Nu Kua – The Bearers of Civilization

Others tell of Fu Hsi and Nu Kua. Unborn, appearing when yin and yang formed the Heaven and the Earth, human-headed, snake-tailed, brother, sister, they lived upon K'un-lun Shan (mountain). There were no human beings then. So Nu Kua took up the yellow earth and worked upon it to form human beings. She worked hard but found her energy flagging. In order to complete her work she gave up moulding each human being by hand and, instead, drew a cord through the clay and from the droplets on the cord created human beings. This is why some people seem to be blessed and have all they need, while others are but poor shadows of the rich and powerful.

Others say she drew her cord through water and shook the droplets off, forming people. Again, it is said, those formed thus were weak and foolish in comparison to the ones formed by hand. This is why inequality exists amongst the black-haired people.

Amongst the demi-gods on earth in those days were two giants, Chuan Hsu and Kung Kung. Both were courageous and fearless. Both adored the battle. Both hated each other. Their battles raged over the earth, taking the lives of many of the peoples made from the droplets from Nu Kua's cord.

At last they fought a final battle. Their swords flew to left and right, splitting mountains, slicing through trees as if grass. Kung

Kung was mortally wounded and fled the battle site. Blinded by blood, Kung Kung stumbled and fell, and as he fell he struck against Pu Chou Mountain causing it to split. Now Pu Chou Mountain held up one quarter of the sky. Great were the disasters unleashed. The sun disappeared from sight as the canopy of Heaven tilted. Rain poured through the gash created by the collapsing pillar of the sky. In darkness and in downpour, with the very heavens falling upon them, the peoples of the earth cried out in horror.

Nu Kua heard their call. Nu Kua saw the damage. Hastening to Pu Chou Mountain she caught a giant turtle. Killing it she took its four feet and upon them planted the supports of the sky. To repair the rent in the sky she needed to find the perfect stone to fit the gap. Knowing this would take some time, she killed a black dragon and stuffed his body into the hole. Then she set off to hunt for the perfect stone. Month after month went by but she found nothing. The body of the dead dragon began to sag under the weight and pressure from the rain attempting to break through. When it seemed as if the makeshift repair would hold no longer, Nu Kua found, deep inside a mountain, the perfect stone, radiant in quality and possessed of an inner spirit. Using fire she carved the stone to be the exact shape. Then she lifted it to the heavens at just the moment when the dead dragon's body collapsed. Waters poured through. Nu Kua heaved the stone upon her shoulder and battled her way through the raging torrents. Water poured over her and she could barely see or breathe. But on she struggled, against overwhelming odds. On she struggled, despite the waters. On she struggled until at last she had the stone in place. Thereupon the waters ceased. The sky righted itself, firm upon its new pillars. The sun rose again and the people of the world rejoiced and sang the praises of Nu Kua, sky mender.

Other stories tell that in the beginning there were no human beings. Fu Hsi and Nu Kua talked in ashamed terms about wedding, even though they were brother and sister. To seek guidance Fu Hsi went with Nu Kua to the very peak of K'un-lun Shan and there prayed:

Heaven, if you wish us to venture forth as man and wife,
let the smoke from our sacrifice hang over the offering.
If this is not what is right, let it be scattered.

The smoke hung over the sacrifice.

One day, when Fu Hsi was the August One upon Earth, he looked up and observed the phenomena of Heaven. He looked down and observed the shape of Earth. He noted the distinguishing features of all beings, birds and beasts alike and how they were suited to their habitat. Some inspirations he took from study of his own body and then went on beyond this to draw further ideas from other things. In this way did he invent the eight trigrams in order to understand the virtues of the spirit world and illustrate the conditions of all that exist in the physical world.

Shen Nung – The Farmer God

In the early times, people knew nothing of which plants to eat, which fruits to pick or where to go for clean water to drink. The result was great suffering, death and hardship.

The Farmer God Shen Nung came to show the people what was safe to eat and drink. He taught the people how to select the five grains from the others. He showed them how to treat the land and which soils to use – separating the good from the bad. He taught them to distinguish between the marshes and the fertile plains; between lowlands and highlands. He himself tasted every plant and every seed to determine whether they were good to eat or not. It is said that in pursuit of this knowledge to help the people, Shen Nung regularly suffered from poisoning; on one day alone, he poisoned himself seventy times!

Shen Nung took wood, split it and made the first plough, inspired it is said by the hexagram Advantage.

Using his tools of agriculture, the Farmer God Shen Nung thrashed every plant and thereby learnt their qualities; their strengths and weaknesses; whether they were sweet or bitter, good or bad. This knowledge he gave to the people and thus is revered as the Farmer God.

Fu Hsi, Nu Kuan and the mysterious Shen Nung are honoured to this day for giving to human beings knowledge of agriculture, medicine, hunting, fishing, music, divination – most especially the eight trigrams of the I Ching. From these Three August Ones came civilisation.

The Grand Mother of T'ai Shan

But others tell of another couple who dwelt upon T'ai Shan, the most sacred of sacred mountains. Here lived the God of T'ai Shan and his sister or, some say, his wife, the Goddess of the Azure Clouds. From T'ai Shan, from this couple, yin and yang manifest, came all life. Down T'ai Shan flowed all creatures, all plants, all life. From here also came the first men and women, not created by the god and goddess, but flowing from their intermingling of yin and yang.

Over the millennia, Emperors have come as Sons of Heaven to worship at the shrine of the goddess. Here they acknowledged where their title of Son of Heaven came from, from the goddess of Heaven, their Mother. And to this day, women seeking children climb the steps to the peak to worship at the shrines of The Old Mother, the Grandmother of T'ai Shan.

Heaven – the Mother of all things

Everything in the universe comes out of Nothing,
Nothing – the nameless
is the beginning;
While Heaven, the mother
is the creatrix of all things.
All mysteries are Tao, and Heaven is their mother.
She is the gateway and the womb-door.
Tao exists, Tao is
but where It came from I do not know.
It has been shaping things
from before the First Time,
from before the Beginning of Time.

The Yellow Emperor – The Bringer of Order

The Yellow Emperor Huang Ti ruled when the world was young. His birth was a sign to those who could see. His mother was standing one night at her window. Suddenly a great flash of lightning lit up the sky and the star Chou of the Great Bear constellation was seen to be surrounded by a halo of light, so great that the land around her was illuminated as if by the rising sun. Immediately she found herself to be pregnant.

For two years and one month she carried the child within her. When Huang Ti was born he spoke straight away. His visage was that of a dragon; his virtue that of a sage. Growing to manhood he

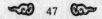 47

became the First Emperor. He came after the Forebearers of Civilisation, Fu Hsi, Nu Kua and Shen Nung. The Yellow Emperor shared the world with his younger brother the Flame Emperor, Yen Ti. Though each had half the world, they each desired to rule the whole world.

The time came when the issue must be decided by warfare. Upon the wastes of Pan Chuan they met. The Fire Emperor drew down flames and fire to his aid. The Yellow Emperor replied with rain and floods. Back and forth across the plains they fought, fire against water, rain against heat. Blood flowed in all directions and it seemed nothing could swing the battle in the Yellow Emperor's favour.

Then did Huang Ti put horn to lip and summon the aid of the beasts and birds. Out of the woods came the bears. Wolves bounded across the wastelands. Panthers descended from the mountains, tigers flew out of the forests, all intent upon coming to Huang Ti's aid. From the sky came flock upon flock of the great hunting birds. Eagles from atop snowy mountains; fighting pheasants from the fields; falcons and kites from the plains. Swirling and wheeling they formed the banners of the vanguard of the Yellow Emperor's army as it swept over the ground towards the fiery hosts of the Fire Emperor.

The battle was long and hard. The bloodshed terrible but necessary. At last Huang Ti overcame Yen Ti and slew him there upon the plains of Pan Chuan. Huang Ti was now undisputed ruler of all below Heaven.

Huang Ti took as his minister Chih Yu. Ox-headed, his horns sharp and deadly, the very hair on his head was as sharp as swords. Great were his skills, greater still his treachery. A rebel he became, traitor to his ruler. Envious of his Master's rule, Chih Yu drew others both on earth and in Heaven to his side with false words and vain promises. When rebellion broke out, the Yellow Emperor took the field against his opponent. He called to him those who would defend the Way of Heaven. To him came the Winged Dragon, while to Chih Yu came the Count of the Winds and the Master of the Rains.

When the armies clashed, the Count of the Wind drove storms into the path of the Yellow Emperor while the Master of the Rains poured down torrents of rain. Back and forth the battle raged for many days until it seemed Huang Ti would break through. Then did Chih Yu summon dank, dark mists to hide himself within. But the Yellow Emperor invented the compass and, with its aid, found his way through the fog and battle commenced again. Chih Yu begged the Master of the Rains to do more to prevent his defeat. The Master drew upon all the forces at his disposal and assaulted the earth with deluges of rain. The Yellow Emperor began to despair for his troops and so he summoned his daughter, clad in green, from her palace on Related Brothers Mountain.

Huang Ti begged his daughter Pa, to launch an attack, for she was the Drought Fury. With her assistant known as the Responding Dragon, she rushed upon the flooding waters and swallowed them up. Then did Pa, goddess of Drought blaze across the land, drying the waters so completely that not a drop remained. With the rains gone, Huang Ti could see Chih Yu clearly. Without his Heavenly forces, Chih Yu was defenceless and fell to Huang Ti's sword. So was the rebellion ended.

But Pa, goddess of Drought had been unleashed. In vain did her father beseech her to return to her Mountain. To this day she is still loose upon the earth, though her powers were contained by her father to the best of his ability.

Fighting the Monsters and Regulating the World

In the courtyard of the Yellow Emperor's Palace grew the kui Yih grass. This grass had remarkable powers. It is said that if a worthless, glib and boastful person entered the Palace seeking his fortune, the grass would rear itself upright and point directly at one such. At the sight of such a condemnation from Heaven, these worthless people fled the Palace.

Far off on the Flowing Waves Mountain, in the depths of the eastern ocean, there lived a monster called Kuei. Ox-like in form, blue in colour, but with only one foot and no horns, it could create storms simply by diving into the ocean. Flashes of light came from it brighter than the sun and moon and its voice created thunder so terrible that the foundations of the mountains shook. The Yellow Emperor saw the distress this creature caused. He watched the waters boil in the storm. He saw the walls shake with the thunder. He determined to put an end to this creature.

With the Winged Dragon he flew far out across the ocean to the Flowing Waves Mountain. Here he captured the Kuei and slew it. From its hide he made a drum upon which he beat with a thigh bone of the Kuei. The sound resounded across five hundred miles and struck awe into all who heard.

The world the Yellow Emperor inherited after his final battle with the Fiery Emperor was one of injustice. The gods and spirits had become bold and treated the earth as their play place. Violence, distrust and dishonesty were rife. From his palace on Kunlun Mountain, he watched over the world and dispensed justice. From his central point he could see all that went on and his power became very great, now that none dare face him.

But there were still lawless elements loose in the world. Worst of these were those gods who used their powers for crime, violence and intimidation. The Yellow Emperor was called upon many times to deal with such deities or spirits. Though he dispensed justice, he could do little to control the powers of such deities, other than to make it clear that they had fallen from grace.

The Emperors of the four directions drew together and plotted against him. The four Emperors each stirred up their own region against the Yellow Emperor. Then at a given time they all four converged on Kunlun Mountain and laid siege to the city and palace.

The Yellow Emperor was moved by the plight of his people, crushed by the enemy. He took no pleasure in war or violence, but the effect of his ignoring the attacks of the four Emperors was that the ordinary people suffered. Sighing, the Yellow Emperor realized that he would have to take the field against them if peace and justice were to return to the lands between the four seas. So it was that the Yellow Emperor brought together his troops and led them in person against the four Emperors. They were soon routed and executed and then did all regions of the world acknowledge the suzerainty of the Yellow Emperor.

One day the god Ku, a half human, half dragon deity, with the god Chin Pi determined to attack a little deity called Pao Chiang, a harmless god who had in some way annoyed them. This crime took place in the vicinity of Kun lun Mountain and the Yellow Emperor was mightily angry. As soon as the crime was reported to him he despatched two officers to arrest and sentence the two murderous gods. They were duly tried and executed. But at the moment of their physical death, they underwent transformations. Ku turned into a terrifying looking bird, eagle-like but vast. With great creaking, dry wings, he swept off across the sky, bringing drought and death in his wake. To this day he sallies forth, flying low across the land and destroying the crops.

Chin Pi changed into a vicious bird as well. He appeared to be like a hawk or osprey, but his hands became tiger's claws. This fearsome creature can be heard to cry out and be glimpsed when war is about to ravage a land.

Yet another tale tells of the troubles of that strange time at the beginning of time.

The god Erh Fu, human of face, serpentine of body, dwelt with his servant near to Kunlun Mountain. The servant was a man of evil thoughts and deeds, who by steadily dripping poisonous thoughts into the ears of Erh Fu turned him against a neighbouring god, Ya Yu. One night, Erh Fu rose up and smote Ya Yu, killing him outright. The Yellow Emperor heard of this crime and sent his officers to arrest both Erh Fu and the evil servant. The servant was put to death, but it was recognized that Erh Fu had been misled. Therefore Erh Fu was not sentenced to death but to long lasting torment. His feet were locked in a stock while his hands were tied together behind a vast tree on the top of Shu shu Mountain. His hair was wound into the very branches of the tree itself. And here he remained for a thousand years until he was found again and released at last from his torment.

But stranger still was the fate of the victim, Ya Yu. The Yellow Emperor took pity upon the poor god and summoned shamans from afar to bring him back to life. The women shamans worked their spells and brought back his spirit from the Land of the Yellow Springs where the dead dwell. But while he was able to return to life, the experience had destroyed his original nature. He became a twisted and bitter creature. Eventually, despising all company, he took up his abode in a deep pool at the base of Kun lun Mountain. From this pool he would leap out upon those foolish enough to pass by unarmed or unprotected. Seizing his victims, he would drag them down into the pool and devour them. It was some time before a just end could be made of this monster, and the tormented soul within be released.

Many were the struggles of the Yellow Emperor. Slowly, slowly did he bring the world into order. He taught the people the arts of war and the skills of peace. He was the first ruler and he followed the Tao. Always eager to understand, he sought out sages and immortals who gave him guidance. His rule was just, his laws impartial. He taught the black haired peoples filial piety and he offered Heaven obeisance and honour. From him flowed the wisdom of kingship and when the time came for his life to end, he did not die. Instead a dragon descended from Heaven and mounting upon it, Huang Ti ascended, leaving his people grieving below.

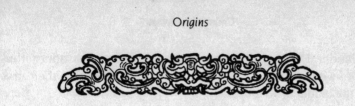

Chuan Hsu – Separating Heaven and Earth

From the Yellow Emperor a mighty family sprang, some good, some bad. His son Chang Yi committed most terrible crimes and was banished to the furthest West. His son, the grandson of the Yellow Emperor, was born hideously deformed, having the face of a human but the feet of a pig. But with Chuan Hsu, great-grandson of the Yellow Emperor, virtue returned to the family and a worthy successor to the famous ancestor was born.

Chuan Hsu was appointed god of the North and went to assist his uncle the god of the West, Shao Hao, rule over his kingdom of birds. This training with the god of the West prepared him for his role as Emperor of the Black haired peoples.

When Chuan Hsu inherited the Empire from the Yellow Emperor, it was at war with the demi-god Chih You and the fierce Miao people. The rule of the Miao people under Chih You was most terrible to behold. Disorder, chaos, violence, break up of civilization and famine stalked the lands under the control of the Miao and Chih You. In those days there was a ladder between Heaven and Earth. This meant that the gods and humans mixed too freely and their distinctions were blurred, leading to interference, the one by the one.

Chuan Hsu observed all that was happening, the distress, the violence and the confusion caused by the two worlds being too close. He thought and he discussed with the wise ones. He saw that easy access between the gods and the humans was not good for either.

Chuan Hsu resolved to change this and to break the physical links between Heaven and Earth. While Chuan Hsu fought and defeated the vile god Chih You and utterly exterminated the hated Miao people, he ordered the two gods Chung and Li to cut down the ladder. He fixed that Chung should destroy the ladder from above, while Li should attack it from below. They did their task and the ladder is no more.

Chuan Hsu was determined that the people should learn to live according to the proper regulations and rules of behaviour. Once he found a brother and sister living together as husband and wife. He sentenced them to be taken deep into a forest, vast and wide, and high upon a mountain range. Here they were to be abandoned to their fates. Here they sought to survive, but under the snow there was no food and the trees were bare. They each died held in the embrace of the other – lovers even in death. A god-bird flew over them and saw their faithfulness even unto death. It swept down and covered their bodies with immortal grass.

Seven years passed and the two lovers returned to life, only they had been transformed into one being, a manlike creature with two heads, four arms and four legs. From this being came the tribe known as the Mengshuang.

Many strange tales are told of the sons of Chuan Hsu. Some say that he had three sons, each of which became ghosts spreading disease. The first became the Fever Ghost; the second a Water Ghost and the third haunts the houses of the city and scares children.

Others say he had a son called Tao Wu who was a terrifying sight and hunted humans. His appearance was that of a tiger but of immense size, with fur two feet long. With a human face and a pig's mouth it resembled Chuan Hsu's own father in part, except that it had the claws of a tiger, tusks of a boar and a tail eighteen feet long. This creature haunts the wilderness areas and brings terror and troubles to many peoples.

Yet another tradition claims that it was Chuan Hsu who fought the giant god Kung Kung and slew him upon the battlefield, causing his head to fall against Ou Chou Mountain, thus bringing down the canopy of Heaven and for ever altering the orientation of the Earth, which is why the sun, moon and stars tilt to the northwest and the rivers silt up in that region to this day.

2

The Yin and Yang Cycles

The Cycle of Yi the Archer

Yi and the false suns

In the time of the Emperor Yao, who first brought together the black headed peoples and created unity and harmony, there arose many strange and terrifying troubles upon the earth. From across the empire came tales of monsters. There was the awful dragon-headed beast, the Chisel-Toothed creature, the Giant Snake and many others. Yao saw all this and was perturbed.

One day, in the twelfth year of his rule, the Emperor Yao was walking in his capital city when he saw coming towards him a young man with a bow and arrow. Kowtowing before the emperor, the young man boasted that he was the finest archer in all the lands of the black headed people, and that he had magical powers which enabled him to fly upon the wind.

The Emperor was duly impressed but decided to test how good this young archer really was. Pointing at a distant pine tree atop a mountain, Yao asked the mysterious archer to fire at it.

The archer notched his arrow. The archer drew back his bow. The archer loosed the arrow, which flew straight and true into the pine. Then he mounted upon the wind and flew to retrieve the arrow.

The Emperor congratulated the young man and gave him the title Yi the Archer and appointed Yi as one of his ministers.

Not long after this, Yao sent Yi to deal with the monsters. The Giant Snake was despatched with a single arrow to its right eye. The Chisel-Toothed creature was trapped and slaughtered and the dragon headed beast, whilst it fought hard, was killed by an arrow to the heart. Yi became the hero of the country and was duly rewarded for his efforts.

One day reports reached Yao of a fearsome wind god known as Fei Lien, a rebel against the just rule of the Son of Heaven and oppressor of the lands over which he moved. Yi was immediately despatched with a troop of three hundred soldiers. Arriving in the lands devastated by the wind god, Yi ordered that large sheets of cloth be hung before every house and anchored by stones. When Fei Lien passed over the land again, the sheets rebuffed his winds and caused the wind god to change direction.

Yi the archer saw this. He mounted upon his own magic wind. He flew to the top of a mountain. From here he saw all. He saw a vast yellow and white bag at the base of the winds. The bag heaved as the winds were exhaled. Yi drew an arrow. Yi notched the arrow. Yi fired. The arrow struck the bag which immediately reverted to its true shape, that of the monstrous god Fei Lien. The god scuttled into a cave to hide, all the while daring Yi to attack the Mother of the Winds. But Yi was not deterred. Yi drew an arrow. Yi fired his arrow. The monster collapsed clutching its knee and begged for mercy. This Yi granted, but only once he had obtained the promise of Fei Lien that he would never again abuse his powers as the wind god. From that day on, the winds were never to be the cause of such damage again.

Now a new and even more terrible trouble arose. One morning the sun rose as usual and its yang energy spread out across the cold earth. The people awoke and were transfixed. For behind the sun came another sun. At first the people rejoiced to have more warmth. But then another sun arose, and another and yet another. As the astonished people watched, ten suns rose over the horizon, each as bright and fiery as the first. The people took cover to escape the scorching heat. The cattle cried in distress and birds fell down in a faint from the sky itself. Respite only came when the suns sank below the horizon at dusk.

The next morning, the people watched with fear as the sun rose again. For a brief moment they thought all was well, but the tip of the second sun appeared and soon the sky was ablaze with the combined yang of the ten suns.

Day after day the suns rose. Day after day the waters in the lakes dried up; the rivers ran dry and the crops withered and burned in the heat. The people were in despair and the Court of the Emperor Yao were at a complete loss.

Then Yao ordered Yi the Archer to attend upon him. He commanded that Yi go and investigate what was causing this disruption of the balance of nature. So Yi travelled to the West River and on Lin Shan he stood and watched as the nine false suns rose, one after the other, following the true sun.

Yi stared. Yi examined. Yi gazed steadfastly into the very heart of the false suns. Using his magical powers he looked to the very essence of the false suns. And what he saw made him smile. Yi drew nine arrows. Yi planted them in the soil before him. Yi took one up and notched it. Yi drew back his bow and the arrow sped towards the first false sun. The arrow sank into the brilliant light and disappeared. Suddenly the sky was torn by an explosion and the light of the first false sun went out. Those watching saw nothing at first, so bright was the glare caused by the explosion. Then they saw a vast black bird tumble from the sky, transfixed by Yi's arrow. Swiftly Yi notched the remaining eight arrows. One after another they streaked across the sky. One by one they disappeared into the glare of the false suns. One by one the suns exploded. From the sky fell eight more black birds, pierced by the arrows of Yi the Archer.

The next morning the people watched. The sun crept over the horizon. The people watched. The sun rose. The people watched.

The sun sailed clear into the sky. The people watched. And no more suns appeared.

Seeing this, the people hailed Yi as the greatest hero and praised Yao as the true Son of Heaven, balancer of yin and yang, harmonizer of the world. And it was then that envy entered the heart of Yi.

Yi of the Sun and Heng O of the Moon

Not long after, the river at Kao Liang rose to dangerous levels. Yi was sent to deal with this. Riding beside the raging torrent, Yi loosed an arrow into the heart of the turbulent stream, which immediately fell back to its source leaving the river bed almost empty. There Yi saw a man, clad in white, mounted upon a fine horse, followed by a retinue of attendants. Yi drew his arrow. Yi loosed his arrow. The arrow struck the man in his left eye and he turned and fled. As the retinue scattered in confusion, Yi espied a beautiful woman in their midst. Yi chose his arrow well. Yi fired his arrow truly. The arrow lodged in the woman's hair. Falling down before him, the woman, whose name was Heng O, sister of the water god Ho Po, thanked him for sparing her life, and offered to be his wife. Yi and Heng O were duly married, little realizing what trauma lay before them.

Yi returned to the Court with his new wife. But in his heart stirred rebellion. He resented the acclaim of Yao by the people. He longed to rule in his stead.

One day, the Emperor Yao and Yi the Archer were riding on top of Ch'ing Yun Shan when they saw an extraordinary bright light shoot across the heavens. It was in fact the trail left by the journey to visit her mother of the third daughter of the Queen Mother of the West, great Goddess of Heaven. Yi mounted upon his cloud. Yi rode to Heaven and found himself on the magic mountain of Lo Fou. But his way was barred by a great door, in front of which stood a monster of terrifying proportions. Seeing this intruder, the monster called the giant birds of the air to fall upon Yi and tear him limb from limb.

With hideous cries, talons extended, the massed flights of birds bore down upon him, while up started the monster. Yi was not worried. Yi notched his arrow. Yi fired his arrow and the monster fell to the ground and the birds fled. The door itself swung wide to admit him. Entering, Yi found himself confronted by none other than the Queen Mother of the West. Upon her head she wore the sheng headdress, about her were her attendants. Her visage was fierce and yet her demeanour was calm, for she knew her power and Yi knelt before her to explain what had drawn him hither.

The Queen Mother of the West explained the arrival of her third daughter and invited Yi to dine with her. At the table, emboldened by her friendship, Yi asked a favour of her.

'I have heard that you know how to create the pill of immortality. I pray you, grant me one that I might live for ever.' For he knew if he had this power, the people would be bound to make him Emperor once Yao had died.

The Queen Mother of the West smiled at this request and said:

'I have heard that you are a gifted architect. Build me a palace on that distant peak and I shall grant your request.'

Yi eagerly agreed and together they travelled to the peak, White Jade-tortoise Mountain where Yi designed her a palace of outstanding beauty. With the aid of the spirits of the mountains and the gods of the court of the Queen Mother, Yi built her a palace beyond all palaces. Its walls were of purest jade; only the most fragrant woods were taken for its timbers. Glass stretched across its roof and the floors were covered with finest marble.

Aided by the gods and spirits, the palace was ready within sixteen days. The Queen Mother of the West was delighted and fulfilled her promise. She called Yi to her. He approached. He bowed. He looked her steadfast in the face. She handed him a pill of immortality, wrapped in silk.

'This will bestow immortality upon you as well as the power of flight.'

Yi was about to depart when she called him back. He knelt again and she spoke.

'But beware Yi the Archer, would-be Emperor. You must not consume it now. You must undergo a spiritual regime of twelve months of special diet and exercises, for to do otherwise will mean the pill will have unforeseen consequences. Do not forget this, Yi the Archer, would be Emperor.'

So Yi returned home. He hid the precious pill in the rafters of his home and told no one, not even his wife. And immediately he began the special regime of diet and exercises designed to prepare him for the gift of immortality.

Not long after his return, another monster appeared in the land and Yao sent for him to deal with it. Yi packed his bow and set off, leaving his wife behind him.

Days extended into weeks and weeks into months. Heng O was lonely and if truth be told a little resentful of her husband. He was so often away. He had also become very aggressive recently and she feared for him and for the Emperor. Not fully understanding what stirred in his heart, she knew enough to know his disquiet and jealousy, while she knew he also loved the Emperor.

Then one day, wandering for lack of anything else to do, she saw a strange light coming from the rafters. Climbing up to investigate she found the pill wrapped in its silk. She immediately realized what it was and why her husband had obtained it. Fearing that immortality would make him so powerful it would corrupt him and destroy what was good within him, she determined to hide the pill. But at that very moment Yi returned home from his latest exploit. Startled by his sudden arrival and appearance, Heng O swallowed the pill. Yi saw what she did and leapt forward with a terrible cry. But too late. Heng O had started to rise up from the ground, her body now able to fly. Yi sprang towards her, but she drifted out of the window, no longer in control of where she went or what she did.

Yi summoned his cloud, but it was too late. Heng O was far, far away by now, rising higher and ever higher. Her uncontrolled flight took her to the very moon where she landed. Suddenly she was overcome with nausea and threw up the covering of the pill as a white phlegm. This transformed itself before her very eyes into a jade white rabbit, who has been her constant companion ever since. Heng O took up her abode on the moon making the pill of immortality from the magic tree that grows upon the moon and special Heavenly minerals of the moon, aided by the rabbit of the moon. To this day the people of China venerate her as Sheng O, Moon Goddess. It is said by some that with the arrival of Heng O, the moon acquired its yin character, female and cold.

But what of Yi? His cloud was dramatically blown off course and he found himself on the sacred mountain of the husband of the Queen Mother of the West, the King Father of the East. The King spoke to the fearful and angry Yi.

'You must not resist what has happened. That is Heng O's fate. Yours is to become an immortal. You deserve high praise for felling the nine false suns. This cannot be yours on earth. So, as your wife is the yin in the moon, you shall become the yang of the sun. So all will see that yin and yang, while different and even at odds, are united in marriage.'

So saying he ordered Yi to eat a red cake and to wear a sign of the moon around his neck.

'These will protect you from the heat of the sun, and will also enable you to visit your wife in the moon. However, she will never be able to come to visit you in the sun.'

This is why the moon depends upon the sun for its light, not the other way round. Yi ate the cake and hung the talisman around his neck. He prepared to leave, but the King Father of the East had one last command.

'You do not know the rising nor the setting of the sun. Only the golden bird can teach you this. Like you this bird has within it the principle of yang. Go to the very horizon where the sun rises. There, beneath the tree of dawn you will find the immortal Ling Chen Tzu who has captured the golden bird. Ask him to release to you the bird of the sun and together travel to the great yang itself.'

Yi travelled to utmost east. He found the great tree of the dawn. Beneath sat Ling Chen Tzu and the caged bird. Bowing low,

Yi requested the golden bird in the name of the King Father of the East and the bird was released into his care. Mounting the golden creature, Yi flew to the sun and built himself his own palace.

Then he recalled his love for his wife and flew to visit her. She took fright, but he caught her by the hand and told her she had nothing to fear, telling her of all that had befallen him. So it is that each month, on the fifteenth day of the month, Yi visits her, combining his yang with her yin – which is why the moon glows with such brilliance on the fifteenth of each month.

The Cycle of Yu

The Emperor Yao summons Kun to control the floods

When the August Emperor Yao grew old, he looked around considering whom should succeed him. Yi the Archer was no more upon the earth. Yao regarded his ten sons, none of whom he deemed worthy of ruling all below Heaven, the multitudes of the black haired peoples. Yao feared for his country and for the guidance that it would need once he was gone.

He had been on the throne for sixty years when he began to enquire who could take his place. His chief minister said, 'There is your son Chou who is very clever,' but the Emperor dismissed this suggestion saying, 'Sadly, he is insecure and argumentative.'

The chief minister then suggested the Minister of Works, but Yao said, 'Sadly, he has wonderful ideas when he has no post, is full of solutions and grand plans. But when he takes up a post, nothing comes of these ideas! Look at how troubled we are with these rising floods.'

The Emperor grew more and more disturbed by the rising floods and the continuous downpour of the rains. He lamented, saying, 'Pouring from the four mountains, the floods embrace the mountains and sweep over the hills, threatening even Heaven with their turbulence and leaving the ordinary people in distress. Where can I find a man capable of correcting this disaster?'

To which the court replied that there was one capable of doing this, Kun. So Yao summoned Kun to his palace and charged him with controlling the flood.

Now this Kun was grandson of the Yellow Emperor himself and, when he wished, took the form of a white horse. For nine years Kun undertook this task. Kun looked at the raging floods, battering even at the gates of Heaven. He looked at the myriad black haired peoples and their suffering and his heart strained within him. Being descended from the god Chuan Hsu, great lord of the skies, he felt within him the power to fight the floods. He sought to use his powers to build ditches, channels and high banks to control the flow. But to no avail. No sooner would he have finished some great ditch, or bulwark against the waters, than it would collapse and the waters surge through again. No matter how hard he worked there simply seemed to be not enough earth around to build up the defences. As the years dragged on he began to despair until at last he thought of a plan. A desperate plan, but by then times were desperate, though this cannot excuse his crime.

The waters were rising higher and higher and Kun had reached a state of almost total hopelessness. He knew that in Heaven, in the charge of the god of Heaven, there was a miraculous kind of earth, earth which if sprinkled upon the waters would reproduce itself and thus provide the very substance with which to fortify the land and build up the defences against the flood.

While Kun was wondering what to do, two strange creatures appeared before him. One was a tortoise with just three legs, the other a great horned owl. Together they counselled him to steal the Swelling Soil from the god of Heaven. They taught him how to gain the confidence of the god and thus have revealed to him where the soil was kept. They showed him how to hide the soil and how to evade the guards of Heaven.

Thus did Kun enter Heaven and steal the Swelling Soil. Carrying it hidden in his bosom, he returned to Earth. But his actions did not escape the attention of Heaven. Heaven's sanctity had been disturbed and vengeance had to be exacted. The god of Heaven commanded Chu Yung the god of fire and the executioner of Heaven to take revenge. Kun realized that Heaven was out for vengeance and fled West to the Feather Mountain. But no matter how fast he rode, the fire god travelled faster. As the foothills of Feather mountain came in view, Kun looked behind him and saw Chu Yung almost upon him. Turning and twisting, he vainly sought to escape but Chu Yung was upon him and there, in the foothills of Feather Mountain, the god slew Kun.

The Birth of Yu the Flood Controller

For three years the body of Kun lay on the slopes of Feather Mountain. Neither sun nor rain, frost nor heat decayed his body. No one dared come near except for the shamans who kept watch over him. Then, after three years his belly split open and from it emerged Yu. Then and only then did the shamans perform their dances and Kun was transformed into a vast yellow bear.

Yao chooses Shun the Filial

Yao watched with increasing sadness as Kun proved incapable of saving the world from the floods. When he had reigned upon the throne for seventy years he sought again to find someone to whom he could hand over rule of all below Heaven. Word came to him of a remarkable man, one Shun of the family of Yu.

It is said that Shun's mother found she was carrying a child after she had seen a great rainbow. When Shun was born his parents were horrified. For he was like no other child. His skin was black and his eyes had two pupils each. His face was that of a dragon and his mouth was out of all proportion to the rest of his body. His parents immediately took against him, fearful that he was some kind of evil creature. But if truth be told, it was his father who turned evil. His father was known as the Blind Man. When Shun's mother died, he married again and had a second son, Hsiang. His second wife loathed Shun and passed on this fear to her son. The three of them conspired to kill Shun. Shun had grown to a great height and they were fearful of him.

One day, at the behest of his family, Shun went to repair a barn. When he was up in the rafters working hard, they crept in and stole the ladder. With Shun apparently unable to escape, they then set fire to the barn. As the flames roared upwards they were sure he was dead. But turning back to their house they saw him landing safely in the courtyard clad in bird's work clothing.

On another occasion Shun's half brother tricked Shun into falling into a cesspit so fetid that it seemed impossible that any living creature could survive the diseases and stench of the pit. But again Shun escaped and appeared clean and fresh smelling before his half-brother Hsiang.

Finally they decided upon one last attempt to kill him. The three of them, the Blind Man, the second wife and the half-brother Hsiang set Shun the task of relining the well. When he had descended into the depths of the well to clear it, they crept up upon him and covered the well so that no living human being could escape but would suffocate and die within.

Hsiang, the evil half-brother said, 'Credit for this plot goes to me. I thought of this way to get rid of Shun. So you, Father and Mother, may have his cattle and sheep and his barns, but I shall take his spears and his musical instruments, and his two wives shall become my servants.'

So saying, Hsiang went into the house and entered Shun's quarters. To his total astonishment he found Shun sitting there quietly playing his lute. Hsiang, considerably embarrassed, said truthfully, 'I was just thinking about you!' To this Shun replied in a quiet voice, 'I was thinking of my people. Will you help me govern them?'

For Shun bore no bitterness. He was the truest of filial sons. Despite the attempts of his father, step-mother and half-brother to kill him, he never ceased to show them the greatest respect. When Yao asked his advisers whom he should appoint to succeed him they said,

'There is a man Shun of Yu who is of the common people. His father was wickedly immoral; his step-mother was without sincerity; his half-brother was arrogant. Yet, despite all this, he has remained true to the best principles and through filial piety has taught them to control their evil urges and to live in harmony. So they no longer practise wickedness.'

Thus did Yao hear of this remarkable young man and thus did Yao order that Shun come to the capital. When Yao saw Shun he agreed to his being his successor and gave him his two daughters as his wives, but did not tell Shun of his plans.

After three years, Yao wished to hand over his throne to Shun. He called Shun to him and offered him the throne. But Shun refused, not believing he was either good enough nor capable enough of such an honour. Yao and his ministers pressed him again and again to accept until at last he was prevailed upon by Yao and the people to accept. So it was that Yao passed over his own sons in favour of Shun of the family of Yu.

Yu fights the flood

While the succession of Yao by Shun was taking place, Yu, son of Kun, had been growing. Some say that he took the form of a dragon at will; others that he was the companion of such a creature. Certain it is that he was no ordinary mortal. He married and settled down, but like all others of the black headed people, he and his lands were threatened still by the floods which raged and roared through the land.

It is said that like his father, Yu could take the form of a giant bear. One day his wife was bringing him his food and had come early. Yu was labouring away in the form of a bear, controlling the floods around his own lands and did not realize she was coming. When she rounded the rocks she saw a terrible monster bear. She dropped the food she was carrying and ran screaming. Yu leapt to his feet and took upon himself again his human form and ran after her calling her to stop. But she ran on, out of her mind with fear, praying to the gods for deliverance. Just as Yu was upon her, she stumbled and was transformed into a rock. At the time this happened she was pregnant. Yu sat before the rock and waited. For nine months the rock grew and grew and Yu waited. Then one night the rock split and from it came forth his child, Chi.

Meanwhile, the Emperor Shun observed the state of his country. He saw the common people distressed and dismayed by the ceaseless waters. And he asked who could be commanded to deal with this. His advisers said only one man was capable of this, Yu, the son of Kun.

The Emperor Shun summoned Yu to the capital and Yu left without even having time to say a proper farewell to his family. Shun ordered Yu to struggle ceaselessly against the floods and not to stop until they had been tamed. Yu bowed low and went forth to do as he was commanded.

First he visited Heaven and sought permission from the gods of Heaven to use the miraculous Swelling Soil. The gods of Heaven approved of his humility in marked contrast to that of his father. They gave their blessing through the Order of the god of Heaven who bestowed upon Yu the Swelling Soil.

Upon returning to earth he set himself the task of blocking the springs from which the endless waters flowed. Accompanied by his companion in travail, the Winged Dragon, Yu travelled from one end of the country to the other. Wherever they came upon a spring, they would stop. Then, riding the Winged Dragon, Yu would plunge into the spring. Deep, deep down they would go. The waters would rush at them, yet were unable to halt their progress. Down, down they went, diving into the very heart of the spring until they came to the underground ocean. Once they broke through, they would then take the magic earth and block the spring at its source. Then up, up, they would ride together, Yu and dragon, dragon and Yu. Bursting out of the ground they would leap towards Heaven and then return to earth to travel on to yet another spring. And again, down, down they would go. Deep, deep into the earth, pushing through the chill waters of yet another spring.

It is said that together they blocked over quarter of a million of the springs, leaving only those that fed the fields of the black headed people.

The springs were now controlled, but the waters they had poured out onto the earth still swirled and rushed about, destroying the fields of the common people, washing away the homes of the wealthy and invading even the ancestral and sacrificial temples of the Emperor.

Seeing this, Yu did not rest. Yu took no thought for himself. Yu sat down beside the mighty Yellow River. He fell asleep. In his dreams he saw himself bathing in the Yellow River. The river swelled up and bore down on him, but opening his mouth he drank the river dry. Rising from the river bed he saw a white fox with nine tails, a sign of great blessing, an omen of success. Awaking he stared out over the rushing waters of the uncontrolled river and wondered. As he stared a strange creature emerged from the torrents. Half fish, half man his face was white as a sheet. In his hand he held a chart upon which were marked the eight trigrams by which the Yellow River could be controlled. Some say that a tortoise also appeared at the same time with the eight trigrams and the map of the river etched upon his shell. Yu killed the tortoise and, drying its shell, used it to divine the progress of his work.

Using the mystic map and with guidance from the oracles, Yu turned to controlling the waters upon the face of the earth. Great were the obstacles in his way, for he had to dig a channel for the

Yellow River. Aided by the Winged Dragon whose tail could cut through living rock and who could burrow deep into the yellow soil, Yu worked his way across the land. From the Leaning Tree at the rising of the sun at Nine Fords, through the lands of the Black Teethed Ones and the plains of the Crossed Toes, on past the mountains of the Feathered Men and Naked Clans to the land of the Three Perils, Yu never ceased to work.

He called to his assistance many of the gods of the rivers and the land. Yu summoned the gods to a great assembly on Kuai Chi Mountain. Here he was opposed by the giant Fang Feng who, to show his disrespect, made no effort to arrive at the assembly on time. Upon his coming late, Yu seized him and killed him, striking off his head. Then and only then did the gods decide to assist Yu.

Thus did Yu and Kiu Ling tackle Hua Shan, the mighty mountain which blocked the Yellow River where it swings to turn towards the Ocean. Together they pushed Hua Shan apart, split it down the middle and burrowed under it. In this way was the river able to flow through the gap and on to the sea. To this day you can see the fingerprints of Kiu Ling and Yu on the slopes of Hua Shan.

Yu and his faithful companion the Winged Dragon split open the rocks and created the Dragon Gate, Lung Men. Together they dug the Meng Men pass. Working ceaselessly they built great banks to contain the river. So hard did Yu work that his fingernails were worn to the bone and no hair grew upon his legs. Even though he passed the very doorway to his home and family on several occasions, he never once turned aside to visit them, so intent was he upon defeating the floods.

It was when he was digging the gorge at Lung Men that one day Yu broke through into an incredibly deep cavern, in the heart of the mountain. Venturing forward, Yu could vaguely see a creature at the far end of the cave. He advanced with his sword drawn, and drew closer and closer until he could make out the shape of the creature. To his astonishment he saw that it was a god with a serpent's tail, none other than the Ancestor god Fu Hsi. Bowing low he asked:

'Great Fu Hsi, why are you here? What can I do for you?'

Fu Hsi, first Father of All spoke not a word.

Yu spoke again, 'Lord Fu Hsi, the world is troubled. The people are disturbed. Only I your servant stand between them and disaster. Is it possible you can help me?'

Fu Hsi, bringer of civilization to the black headed peoples, said not a word.

Yu spoke again, 'Divine Fu Hsi, bridge between Heaven and Earth. Is it because we have offended Heaven that they punish us so?'

Then, and only then, did Fu Hsi speak.

'Yu, son of Kun. We have watched your labours. Great is your skill. Mighty is your strength. Dauntless is your desire. Yet even you cannot hope to tame the waters alone. The gods have decided to aid you, which is why I have come. Draw near, son of Kun.'

Yu did as he was commanded and Fu Hsi drew out from the folds of his clothes a beautiful jade tablet, two feet two inches long.

'Yu son of Kun, take this tablet, a gift of the gods. By it Heaven can assist you; through it you can assist the earth. The true measure and depth of all things will be known to you.'

So saying, Fu Hsi disappeared from Yu's sight. Taking the jade tablet, Yu measured and directed all under Heaven.

For ten years he laboured. From the utmost west to the utmost east. From coldest north to steamiest south. On mountains and in the valleys he thought of nothing but controlling the waters; he did nothing but defend the common people. So terrible was the cost to him that his face turned pitch black; his body became twisted and diseased and only with difficulty could he walk. He suffered dreadfully from internal problems and his body shrank by half. Yet he would not rest for one hour until the waters had been tamed.

At long last, after ten years of unremitting labour, the great waters were tamed. Then and only then did Yu rest.

Shun the Emperor saw what Yu had done and was mightily pleased.

The Death of Shun

Shun ruled for many years until he passed away while visiting his southern dominions. At Tsang Wu he died and his two wives, daughters of Yao, drowned themselves, perishing in the waters of Hsiang river where their spirits still move. Beside the Hsiang river is the rare and beautiful speckled bamboo whose stems are dappled with the marks of tears. These, it is said, were so marked by the weeping of the two Queens for their lost Lord. They are known as the Hsiang Queens bamboo.

When Shun was buried at Tsang Wu, it was his half-brother Hsiang who dug the tomb and who mounted guard upon it for the remainder of his life. In this way did the filial love of Shun find its reward in the fraternal devotion of Hsiang.

Yu the Emperor measures and controls the world

Upon the death of Shun, Yu the Great, tamer of the waters ascended the throne.

Now he was master of the black haired people, he set out to measure and understand all that is below Heaven. He raised the four mountains of the compass and regulated the flow of the rivers. He visited and explored the whole of his land, giving number to the people and extent to the fields. He sought constantly to comprehend and to record.

Summoning two of his greatest ministers to him, Ta Chang and Shou Hai, he commanded them to measure the world. Ta Chang paced out the distance between the east and west poles; Shou Hai paced out the distance between the north and south

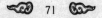

poles. When the two ministers had completed their epic task they reported back to the Emperor.

Ta Chang said, ' I have walked the distance between the east and west poles and have found it to be two hundred and thirty three thousand, five hundred and seventy five paces.'

Shou Hai reported, 'Master, I too have paced the distance between poles, between the north and the south and have found it to be equal to that between the east and west.'

And Yu nodded, pleased that the Earth was harmonized as he had expected.

News came late one year from the east of a terrible monster which was ravaging the lands of the Empire. The creature was known as Hsiang Yao. Its form was that of a serpent with nine heads, so vast that it lay across nine mountains and its vomit was deadly to people, creatures and land alike.

Yu rode forth accompanied by his guards. They rode through lands now at peace. Everywhere Yu went he measured and record ed. At long last he arrived at the site of the nine mountains. The beast reared up, its nine heads looking in all directions at once, making it impossible for any to approach. Espying Yu it brough forth a great flood of venom. Yu leapt upon the back of his faithfu companion, the Winged Dragon. Up, up they soared while the ven om washed over the lands below. Taken by surprise, the beas Hsiang Yao tried to turn round to find where Yu had gone. In al directions did its heads look, save upwards. In all directions did it: evil fumes emanate, except upwards. In all points was it invulnera ble from attack, except from above.

Down, down dived the Winged Dragon, loyal warrior of Yu the Great. Down, down came Yu riding upon its back. Too late, too late did the beast realize the way its foe had gone. Down, down came the sword of Yu. Up, up sprang the life's blood from the necks o the nine heads.

Long and slow was its passing. Great and awful was the pour ing out of its foul blood. Even the very mountains seemed to shrink from the stench and pollution. No living creature, no plant no fish could survive on the lands over which the beast's death cast a pall. Yu and the Winged Dragon dug a great channel into which they heaved the corpse and its effluent. But so terrible was its putridity that it burst from the channel. Next the two companions dug a ditch, twice the depth of the channel. But again the beast, as deadly in death as in life, burst forth again poisoning the lands. Now the two built a great mound and buried the corpse, but yet again, this failed to hold the evil flood.

Finally Winged dragon and Yu the Great dug a vast lake. Into this they threw the body and then buried it under a mountain of earth to form a great island in the midst of the lake. On top of this they built a tower to control the evil of the beast. At last the evil was contained and the land began to return to life.

When Yu had surveyed the whole earth he called for the Nine Shepherds to bring ores from the nine regions of the world. When this had been done, Yu cast the ores and made the Nine Cauldrons. Upon each he emblazoned the symbols, scenery and creatures of the nine regions. By this he was able to hold all that dwells in the nine regions in loyalty to him and to his dynasty. In this way was he able to show how to be true Son of Heaven.

The nine cauldrons were of miraculous form, for as they passed down from ruler to ruler or dynasty to dynasty their weight varied. Thus when Yu handed them over to his son Chi who succeeded him, they weighed so much it took ninety men and oxen to move but one of them. Yet when the Hsia dynasty founded by Yu fell, so venal was the last Emperor that the nine cauldrons could be picked up by any man. Yet when the Shang dynasty fell and the Chou received the Mandate of Heaven to rule, they also received the nine cauldrons. It took ninety thousand men to haul just one cauldron. Heavy when righteous men ruled, the cauldrons became as light as feathers when the morality of the Emperors was drained and corruption had entered the ruling family.

When Yu died, his son took his place. And so it has been ever since that son follows father, except when Heaven withdraws its favour and a new dynasty arises. When Yu died the world had been

3
Confucian

The Loyal city god

Yue Fei lived during the Sung dynasty when the Throne was occupied by a weak and worthless emperor. Yue Fei was born in the year 1103 AD and his birth was presaged by a giant bird which alighted upon the roof of his family's house and spoke with a human voice, foretelling the birth of a worthy one.

His family lived in Hunan and were an example to all. Even though they were not wealthy, they gave all that they could to feed and help the poor. They even went hungry themselves in order to help others. In particular, Yue Fei's mother was a tower of strength to all around her and instilled in her young son the virtues of loyalty and honesty.

Yue Fei grew up as an honourable man and a formidable warrior and archer. In the effete world of the Sung Court, he stood out as a magnificent and devoted exception, using his powers to help keep the Empire together.

Now at that time the Jurchen Mongols were invading, carving out a kingdom for themselves in northern China. In 1126, the Jurchen captured the old imperial city of Kaifeng and the Court had to flee south to Hangchow. Yue Fei, horrified by what had happened but too young to be given command himself, worked night and day to prepare to throw back the invading army. At the age of 37 he raised an army of loyal peasants and marched north to confront the Jurchen.

His battle cry was 'Give us back our rivers and mountains', and with this resounding from their lips he met the Jurchen army and routed the vast horde completely. One might expect that such an action would bring him the praise and thanks of the Court. But these were bad times. The Chief Minister of the Emperor was one Chin Kuei and he and his wife were already in league with the Jurchen. They were prepared to betray their country for money and for power in the new dynasty. Seeing the success of Yue Fei, they began to feed the weak Emperor stories of Yue Fei's supposed arrogance. They bred fears in the Emperor that Yue Fei might try to take over the Empire himself.

Having aroused such fears, they then persuaded the Emperor to order the arrest of Yue Fei on grounds of treason. Yue Fei was shocked when he was arrested and thrown into jail. Here he was tortured upon the instructions of the evil minister and his wife. When at last he was brought to trial, Chin Kuei felt victory near. But Yue Fei confounded them all. When he was asked why anyone should believe he was really a loyal servant of the Sung Emperor, Yue Fei tore off his shirt to reveal four characters tattooed upon his back. They read, 'Loyal even unto death for my country.' These characters, said Yue Fei, were tattooed on his back by his mother before he went to fight his first great battle against the Jurchen.

Suitably impressed by this, the Court let him go. But Chin Kuei had not finished. Yue Fei was asked a second time to return from the front. On his way, the abbot of a monastery warned him not to return to Hangchow, but as the command to return came from the Emperor, Yue Fei would not disobey. Sure enough, Chin Kuei had him arrested on further trumped up charges and then murdered in cold blood in the prison, two days before New Year in the year 1141. The chroniclers of this event say it was pouring with rain throughout that day, as if Heaven itself were weeping bitter tears at this injustice.

In due course of time, the terrible truth was revealed. A new Emperor arose and he studied the evidence before him and exonerated Yue Fei and ordered that the memory of Chin Kuei and his wife be tarnished for all times. Above Yue Fei's tomb was raised a fine temple. And outside where his body actually lay, a set of statues were erected. They show Chin Kuei, his wife and two others implicated in the injustice. Cast in iron, they are bound and kneel in contrition before the tomb. To this day people visiting Yue Fei's tomb spit upon the statues of Chin Kuei and accomplices, so much so that the popular name for a spittoon is Chin Kuei. Meanwhile the citizens of Hangchow petitioned the Emperor and Heaven that Yue Fei be made the City God of Hangchow, which honour he was duly accorded.

The Lost Grave

Every day Chou Fang Yung thought of his father but he could hardly remember his face or his voice. His father, Wen Jung, was an official in the far off province of Hupeh. He had returned to his family home in Huating to marry and his son had been born after one year. But duty called and he had to return to his work. When Chou Fang Yung was five years old his father returned to visit the family for several months but his son only had a vague memory of the visit and consequently little detail. It was to be the last time he saw his father. When Chou Fang Yung was thirteen years old his father died while working in Kueichou in Hupeh province.

Without Wen Jung's income, his widow and son and his elderly parents were left penniless. His widow did what she could to support the family by spinning and weaving and what she earned was

 77

enough to buy food but nothing more. The Chou family had very few males in their family line, there was no man to help with the upkeep of the house and, worse still, no male relative to travel to Hupeh to collect Wen Jung's remains. In order to prevent the dead man's soul from wandering aimlessly they held ceremonies to invoke his soul to return safely home. They did their best but were troubled that the funerary rites were not complete.

Not long after this bereavement Chou Fang Yung's grandparents also died. In their last moments of life they had begged their young grandson not to forget his father. 'It is your filial duty to search for the dead man and return his body,' they said, 'so we can all rest in peace.' Their dying words created a deep impression on the young boy and he vowed never to forget his duty.

In the years that followed the family became even more destitute. But Wen Jung had an important skill, he was a talented calligrapher and artist. The money gained from his services provided meagre food and fuel but how could he save enough to make the journey in search of his father? Each year he promised himself that he would start his search but he could not leave his mother without any support.

Early one summer, as he and his mother carried out rites in memory of their ancestors, Wen Jung was deeply upset to see his mother shaking with grief. 'Whatever the cost to my physical health,' he vowed, 'I will make the journey and restore honour to my family.' Over the following months he adhered to a strict and simple vegetarian diet and wore the cheapest, coarsest cloth. Whatever money he saved was put aside to support his mother during his absence.

On his last day at home he offered incense at the family shrine and knew he would not return until he had his father's remains with him. The money he had saved had all been given to his mother and the journey to Hupeh was too dangerous and arduous to undertake without financial backing. And so Wen Jung started for Peking to offer his services to the retinue of any official bound for Hupeh province.

 78

In order to pay for his passage on a rice-bearing boat to the capital he drew delicate paintings. During the days it took to reach their destination he practised his brush strokes and acquired the skill of drafting official letters. By the time he reached Peking he felt sufficiently confident in his abilities to offer his services to a government delegation. He immediately set about contacting men of influence from his home town, men who might speak on his behalf to employers. He told his contacts about his mission to find the remains of his father, of his vow never to return home until he had done so, and of the efforts he had made to secure finances for his mother. The men from his home town of Huating were so impressed by his devotion that they called him Chou the Filial Son and they promised to speak on his behalf whenever possible.

As the months passed in Peking none of the recommendations bore any fruit; for an unknown reason it seemed that Chou would not make the journey to the city of his father's death. He returned to his contacts in Peking and although they reassured him that many official delegations left for Hupeh no-one could explain why he had not been offered work.

Chou felt that time and money were running out. He had pawned his belongings to pay for a small room at an inn but the New Year was approaching and the innkeeper needed all bills to be settled. Then, by chance, he heard that Mr Keng, a neighbour of his family, had arrived in Peking. Chou called on him to put his case forward and was promised help after the New Year. He dutifully returned to Mr Keng's lodgings in the first month of the New Year and was taken into a room where other men from Huating had gathered. Amongst them was Mr Tai, a respected elder who had been his father's colleague in the town of Kueichou. He fell on his knees before this man, his first real link with his father, and implored him to say where his father's coffin might be buried.

Chou's pleas had taken the group by surprise and they listened with interest as Mr Keng told the group the story of young Chou. Mr Tai was first to speak:

'Yes, I knew your father well. He would be proud to see how his son has grown and impressed by your filial duty. You are a learned young man but you have no money. There are mountain ranges, endless plains and turbulent rivers between here and Kueichou. There are also problems in the city itself. For years it has been ransacked and burnt by rebellion, its houses destroyed, its residents have scattered and its graveyards been turned over. How can you ever find the temporary grave of our father? Your father would admire your devotion but do not forget that you have a mother who needs you, it is also your filial duty to care for her. My advice is to return to a mother who is watching for you at the door. I will listen for information on your behalf.'

Chou put his head in his hands and wept. He and his ancestors could never be at peace until he had found his father. He looked up at M. Tai:

'Thank you for your offer but I can never give in. If I have to I will walk every step of the way begging at every village, eating scraps that are thrown away.'

The old men of the town could not help but admire Chou the filial son who would not rest until he had performed his duty. Mr. Tai promised to write him a letter of introduction to the chief constable of Kueichou, an old acquaintance of his. Everyone in the room decided to contribute something towards the young man's trip. The following day young Chou collected a purse of money, a letter of introduction and a detailed itinerary for the trip which Mr Tai had prepared for him.

Chou returned to his lodgings to gather his meagre belongings and it was there that he met another young man who had been doorkeeper to a country magistrate. His experience in the courts and beyond had given him good contacts with government officials between Peking and Nanking and his new friend suggested they travel together.

'You are a stranger to these parts, Chou. But I have come to know many people and can help you with the necessary introductions. We could form a useful partnership; you can paint scrolls and write letters and I can provide contacts. Once you have arrived at Nanking you can catch a boat which will take you closer to your destination.'

The two men set out together the next day. Chou's fine brush-work was a pleasure to the eye, his travelling companion paid his respects to his contacts, and somehow they survived. Halfway through their journey they stopped at a customs barrier and his travelling companion went in search of an old friend, leaving Chou alone in a strange town. As he sat in the inn an overwhelming feeling of anxiety and sadness came over him and he decided to contact a teacher from his home town. It would take eight days to reach the city where the teacher lived, 'but I have travelled so far for so long,' he thought, 'another journey doesn't matter. The teacher might help me find the quickest way to Hupah.'

Chou found a passage on a small boat and slept on the deck, barely eating and victim to the elements that tossed the boat. For months he had been subject to extremes of hunger, cold and heat. He had slept in wet clothes, been burnt by the sun as he travelled shadeless roads and spent days surviving on water and a handful of rice. By the time he left the boat and found lodgings he had been consumed by a fever. He was only halfway to his destination but Chou was engulfed by the illness, unaware of the time or the place.

At that time the area had been hit by a plague and hundreds were dying. The innkeeper did not want to be left with this unknown man lying in his inn and decided to abandon Chou at a nearby temple where he would die. Through his illness Chou had not lost sight of his mission, aware that his determination to succeed would keep him alive, and he begged the innkeeper to call the headman of the street.

The headman duly arrived and like all those who had heard the story before was astonished by the young man's discipline and bravery. Chou showed him the letter of introduction and the purse of money given to him by the old men of the town.

'I know I can survive,' pleaded Chou. 'Use this money to pay for a physician and for my burial if I should die. If anyone from my home town of Huating should pass through here, please tell them where my coffin lies.'

The headman could not refuse this request and called the services of a physician, who, by chance, was a friend of the teacher Chou had been seeking. When the physician heard the story he, too, vowed to make every effort to help the young man. The physician ground herbs and plants to make potions to soothe the fever and in the morning, midday and evening he cared for Chou. After fourteen days the young man had recovered but his body was still weak. He felt a renewed sense of urgency and once more made preparations to resume his journey, but his body could not fight off the cold and once more he had a relapse. Three more weeks passed before finally Chou completed the journey to Mr. Chi, the teacher. When he turned up at his door the young man could hardly stand, his tattered clothes hung limply across the bones on his chest and shoulders.

Mr. Chi took Chou into his home, gave him a mattress to rest on and warm medicinal soup. He, too, saw the determination in the young man's eyes, but begged him to stop the journey and return home. 'You have more than fulfilled your duty to your father,' he said, 'and now it is time to fulfil your duty to your mother.' But Chou had come so far he could not stop.

For several days Chou accepted the hospitality of the teacher and in return painted scrolls of delicate beauty. Mr. Chi recognized the young man's talent and sent the scrolls to wealthy students asking for their patronage. And so it was that Chou collected twenty taels of silver, enough to furnish him with basic necessities for his onward journey.

The next stage was through wild and barely inhabited forest and mountain. It was in the sixth month of the year and the flies and mosquitoes ran a constant attack on him. The heat wore him down and the humidity continually soaked his clothes. The paths through the mountains were rough and sometimes disappeared. It was hard to know which path was safe from robbers or wild animals, and inns where he could find refuge were scarce.

His woven sandals and clothes began to rot from the humidity or were torn by thorns and bushes. Sometimes he slept under trees or in hollows in the ground. His dreams were troubled and one night he imagined a long, black snake slithered down his neck, twisted across his body and came out of his jacket sleeve. Later one night he thought he saw a pair of lanterns swinging in the darkness, a sign of fellow travellers, but it was the luminous eyes of a tiger ready to pounce. He ran in fear through the undergrowth and threw himself in a ditch, tearing his clothes and scratching his face on the low branches.

On one occasion he joined a group of pedlars, travelling with their wares strung across their shoulders. He felt safe in large numbers but one afternoon several pressed ahead of the group only to be beaten and robbed by bandits. Those who survived returned to warn the others and new routes had to be found through the mountains. Months passed and most of the time Chou was alone, exhausted but watchful, driven on by the thought of his ancestors.

Winter was approaching by the time he reached Hankow and the wind and cold began to bite. He studied the itinerary Mr. Tai had given him in Peking, a detailed account of the route from Hankow to his destination Kueichou. There were rivers to sail up or to cross, and inns or villages where he could find cheap shelter. Chou took passage on small boats but the conditions were harsh and his sleep was fitful and troubled. When he could he sold scrolls or wrote letters and gathered enough cash to make the long ascent up the Yangtze river to the city where his father died.

He was so close to this strange city but still the forces of nature continued to challenge him. On the boat through the steep and unpredictable rapids he dreamt that his father spoke to him, 'Take care as you enter the gorges tomorrow'.

His father's words came true as they hit fast, rough water and were thrown against the rocks as they made their way through. Finally, the boat approached the upper end of the Yangtze gorges and high on the rocks stood the city of Kueichou.

The town, once fortified by magnificent Ming dynasty walls, had been torn by rebellion and the walls destroyed. Wooden ramparts had taken their place but they had been burnt in the clashes. Slowly the city was being rebuilt and had been given new life by the refugees who filled its streets. Businesses were established and trade had picked up but the families and buildings of the past had been pulled apart.

Chou found lodging at an inn near the magistrate's main office and contacted the chief of police. He gave him the letter of introduction that Mr. Tai had written which accordingly won the police officer's support and respect.

'I will do what I can to help but familiar names have been replaced by outsiders. Even those who have always been in our city cannot recall the events of the last ten years. How can we find someone who can tell us the story of twenty years ago? Cemeteries have been destroyed, land dug up and built on, tombs have been turned into foundation stones and names and records lost. I will take you to land outside the city limits where you can wrap a piece of earth in cloth and pray to the ancestors; your father's spirit will hear and you will have completed your duties.'

But although Chou was weak and stooped he burnt with determination. 'I cannot leave now that I am so close to my father,' he insisted. The chief of police took pity on him and ordered a search of the remaining records from temples and buildings where coffins would have been kept. The police scanned records and questioned the old retainers but no evidence that his father had been there came to light.

Weeks passed and Chou searched and waited for news until by chance he met an old policeman who worked for the same magistrate as his father. The old man had come in from the country to visit friends and had turned up at the magistrate's office. Chou respectfully questioned the old man, pushing him for details of the past and the men who worked alongside him.

'I recall the arrival of Magistrate Huang to this town. He had a retinue of three secretaries and amongst them was Mr. Chou. He was ill from a journey they had made and a boy servant took care of him. But there was little we could do and one day the servant sent an urgent message for me to come to him. When I arrived your father was dead, the servant beside him still holding a cup of medicine. I can still remember a few details of your father's manner and appearance but it was all so long ago. We arranged for him to be buried and one of our colleagues attended the funeral and the burial.'

Chou could not move or speak as he listened to the old man. He felt that his journey was coming to an end and the tears that filled his eyes came from the sorrow and joy of hearing someone speak of his father.

'Could you possibly remember where my father was buried?' asked Chou.

The old policeman seemed lost in thought for a while and then replied, 'I cannot be sure, but I think it was outside the East Gate where the merchants and travellers were buried. But so many upheavals have changed the land, I doubt that you will ever find the tomb.'

Chou bowed low in thanks, grateful for this priceless information. He ran to tell the chief of police who in turn sent orders for Captain Hsu to help Chou in his search. Chou spent that night in a temple close to the East Gate and at first light the men made their way through the overgrown cemetery. Many tombstones were missing, others were broken or buried, it seemed a long time since anyone had attended to the spirits of the ancestors. They searched all day, working their way through weeds and bushes that had taken over the land but they found nothing. Chou returned the following day and the day after that.

As dusk fell on the third day Chou promised himself that he would search through the bones and weeds for another 14 days. 'If I fail to find the tomb by the fifteenth day I will throw myself into the rapids at the foot of Kueichou,' he vowed. As he looked up his eye caught the tip of a tombstone enclosed by weeds which had sunk halfway into the ground. He cleared the plants away and read

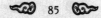

85

the three vertical lines of script and there in the middle line was his father's name, Chou Wen Jung of Huating County. He knelt close to the stone and ran his fingers across the stone, hardly believing what he had found. The date of his father's death was inscribed on the right hand side and the script on the left told how the stone had been erected by his father's friends and colleagues.

Chou lay weeping on the ground that covered his father's body, his hands encircling the precious stone. The old guide who watched over the cemetery heard him weeping and drew close, his lantern lighting up the form of the sad and poorly clothed young man. 'There are wild beasts that prowl this cemetery at night,' he warned Chou.

'I am not afraid of them, I will not leave my fathers' grave!' declared Chou. In the end the guide dragged Chou away from the stone to protect him.

News of Chou's find spread throughout the magistrate's office and they came to express their good wishes. Now he had found his father's grave they believed he would make offerings and return home, he had fulfilled his filial duty. But Chou had one last task to perform and he would not leave the city unless he was carrying his father's bones. How could anyone amongst them stop a man with such devotion? The magistrate who felt deeply for him sent the headman of a local area to help him unearth the bones.

On the ninth day of the ninth moon they arrived to carry out their task. It was a holiday for the people of the city, a time when they went to high land to enjoy the scenery and to picnic, and small groups had gathered around the vicinity of the cemetery. At first few noticed the two men enter the cemetery carrying two jars, oil, incense, cloth, paper and silk, string, pens, tools and tomb offerings. Chou burnt incense and paper money and offered food to his ancestors. They carefully removed the earth surrounding the coffin and lifted the wooden lid, soft and crumbling from the damp earth. There lay the skeleton of his father, his jaw had dropped and his mouth was open. Chou took a knife from his bag and cut the skin from his forearm and laid it over his father's mouth. Chou then sealed his arm with soil from the grave. He gazed steadfastly at the bones of his father and didn't even notice the crowd who had left their picnics and gathered around the grave, amazed by the strength of his filial devotion.

Chou tenderly wrapped each bone in a cloth and made a note of its details. He secured each parcel and then placed it in a yellow bag. He took rubbings of the engravings on the tombstone as proof of the tomb and to reassure his mother that their ancestors could finally rest.

Chou carried his father's bones back to his temple lodgings and laid them in the hall of departed souls. He made eager preparations to return to his mother, confident that sales of his calligraphy and painting would raise enough money to return safely to Huating. He worked with intensity but it was impossible to raise the money he needed. Then something happened that would finally lead him on his journey home. He was selling a scroll to an acquaintance when he was introduced to an influential army officer, General Chang.

Like everyone else who had heard the story, General Chang was entranced by the young man's courage. The General had visited the town for a dinner with local officials and during the meal he recounted the story of Chou the filial son. The local magistrate, attending the dinner, heard how Chou could not afford to take his father's body home. 'I would be ashamed if such an event came to pass in my town,' he declared. He stood up and offered to contribute five taels of silver to the young man, this was soon followed by offers of silver from other officials. Before long twenty taels of silver had been raised and the general himself promised to commandeer a boat which would carry Chou to Hankow.

The following morning Chou heard the good news and called on the magistrate. 'How can I thank you for your kindness to me?' he asked. 'There is something you can do for me,' replied the magistrate. 'Would you copy for me, in your finest calligraphy, passages from the Classic on Filial Piety? These pages, written by a devoted and courageous young man, would be something for me to cherish and my children to inherit.' On bidding his farewell, the magistrate gave Chou a letter addressed to the magistrate of Huating, which contained a full account of Chou's endeavours.

On the twenty-sixth day of the ninth month, Chou boarded the boat for Hankow. In his white clothes of mourning he bowed to the hundreds of people who had gathered to wish him a safe journey. The boat travelled swiftly down the rapids and he watched as the town of Kueichou disappeared into the clouds. Within three days they arrived at Hankow where he changed boats. Two more weeks of travel passed before he arrived at his home town.

He mother had kept watch throughout the months and was overjoyed to welcome her son home. Without delay, mother and son deposited the bones in a temple with the stone rubbings from the tombstone. A place was prepared in the ancestral graveyard and the body was finally buried with the correct funeral rites and offerings.

Chou handed the letter from the magistrate of Kueichou to his local magistrate. Like all those who encountered the young man on his journey, the local magistrate was full of admiration. 'Your devotion,' he said, 'is an example to us all, and I cannot commend you highly enough.' Word spread quickly among the poor and the influential and it was not long before the Chou family were honoured by the Emperor.

Two Brothers and a Mandarin

Like his ancestors before him Chang was born and had married in the province of Shantung. He and his wife were still a young couple when their province was overrun by an invading army and his wife was carried off by soldiers. Chang did not see her again.

Chang had often visited Honan on business and now that he was alone he decided to start a fresh life there. He found a wife who bore him a son they named Na. His second wife died unexpectedly and so Chang took a third wife, a jealous and vindictive woman. She bore a son named Ch'eng whom she cosseted and spoilt, but she treated her stepson, Na, like an animal. Ch'eng was given the best cuts of meat and the finest quality clothes and Na was left with scraps and clothes of coarse fabric. Ch'eng was sent to school and Na was ordered out of the house at dawn to collect heavy bundles of wood. If he failed to find enough fuel she would beat him harshly. As Ch'eng grew older he began to realize what was happening to his older brother and felt a bond of devotion to him. He was aware of his fraternal duty to protect his brother and often complained to his mother about her heartless treatment, but she took no notice.

One day Na returned home late. A storm had broken over the mountain where he had been collecting wood and he had sheltered in a hollow. On his return he was beaten and sent to an outhouse without food. In sympathy, his brother asked a neighbour to bake him cakes which he hid under his coat and smuggled into his brother.

'You mustn't do this for me,' said Na. 'I am not going to die if I am denied an evening meal. Do not put yourself at risk.'

Ch'eng laid a hand around his brother's shoulders. 'But you are forced to work hard and you are not strong. I will help you if I can.'

The following morning Ch'eng followed his brother into the forest and began cutting wood with him.

'Leave me!' begged Na. 'You will be in trouble in school.' But Ch'eng refused.

'You see this hatchet?' cried Na. 'I will kill myself with it if you do not go!' Faced with this threat, Ch'eng reluctantly returned to school. He was beaten by the headmaster for playing truant but refused to say where he had been. The next day Ch'eng followed his brother into the forest again, and once more Na forced him to

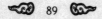 89

go to school. This time he was beaten even harder by the headmaster for playing truant, so Na went to the school himself and told the headmaster the truth. The headmaster was so impressed with young Ch'eng's devotion that he gave him permission to help his brother whenever he wanted.

In the following weeks Ch'eng secretly followed his brother to the forest to work for several hours before going to school. He ignored Na's pleas not to follow him and knew in his heart that his brother was grateful for this support.

One morning they were sitting with a group of woodcutters when they heard a rustle in the undergrowth behind them. They turned to see a tiger leap into the clearing where they sat. The men fled in all directions while Na reached out to protect his younger brother. But it was too late – the tiger had snatched Ch'eng in its sharp teeth and begun its retreat back to the undergrowth. Ch'eng's body was heavy, limiting the tiger's speed, and Na chased it with an axe, slashing at the tiger's haunches. But the tiger disappeared leaving a trail of blood.

Na was desolate and raised the axe to his own throat, bringing it down deeply into his veins. Blood spurted into the air and Na grew faint, his axe dropped to the floor and he became unconscious. The other woodcutters gathered round, stemming the flow with their own jackets and tunics. They bandaged his wound tightly and carried him home on their shoulders.

When he gained consciousness his stepmother stood over him, berating him for the death of her son Ch'eng. Na lay on a straw mattress too weak to speak or move. Waves of pain washed through his limbs, so deep he could neither sleep nor speak. Every now and then, his watchful father crept in to feed him but he, too, was frightened of his wife's wrath. Heartbroken over the death of his brother, Na finally died.

Na's spirit left his body and wandered the streets of Honan. By chance he came upon a local magician who had the power to speak to spirits and call upon devils to act in the mortal world.

'Have you seen my brother? Please take me to him,' he begged.

The magician led Na to the gates of a city full of spirits and devils. As they approached, an official servant was leaving the city carrying the city lists. The magician enquired after young Ch'eng and the servant duly consulted his list of latest arrivals but Ch'eng was not amongst them. The magician would not abandon his quest and the servant felt obliged to check all the lists old and new but Ch'eng could not be found.

Na wandered into the city where he came across the spirits he himself had known from his mortal life but none had seen his brother. Suddenly they were struck by brilliant rays of light, the brightest they had ever known. They looked to the sky and saw the immortal P'u-sa descend on a thick, luminous pillow of clouds. The magician gazed towards this wonderful vision and pulled Na close to him,

'You are very fortunate, Na. This heavenly being full of compassion and mercy only descends once in many thousands of years. He has come today to banish suffering and to free the souls of those in hell.' Na knelt before P'u-sa; all around him devils and spirits were kneeling, singing songs of thanks and praise to the compassionate one who would release them from suffering. P'u-sa held a large willow branch which he used to sprinkle their bodies with water. The bright clouds began to fade and suddenly P'u-sa had disappeared from sight.

Na felt water trickle down his neck, he sensed that the axe wound in his neck had begun to heal and the pain which had plagued him had ceased. The magician led Na gently back to the gates of his village and then left him.

Suddenly, Na woke up on the mattress stained with his own blood. He felt his neck and the wound had disappeared, he looked at the mattress and the stains were dried blood. He eagerly called his parents.

'Ch'eng is not dead!' he assured them, and told them what he had seen. Even though his neck was fully healed his mother rejected his story. 'You are a liar and a murderer!' she cried. His father remained silent in the face of his wife's ferocious temper.

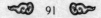

Certain that his brother was not dead, Na vowed to search the world to find him and confided in his father,

'He is my only brother, I must find him. I will not return until we have been reunited. If I do not return you must consider me dead.'

His father wept to be separated from his only surviving son but knew that he could not stand in his way. He gave him a blessing as he said farewell.

Na visited every house, village or town that he came to, pleading for news of his brother. As the months passed Na's clothes became threadbare and the skin of his feet was thick with callouses. To the outsider he had the appearance of a beggar but however often he was scorned he would continue with the same question, 'Have you seen my brother, Ch'eng?'

A year passed and he reached Nanking. The road in and out of the city gate was busy with traffic: peasants and their animals, servants, government officials, hawkers and merchants threaded their way on the dusty road. The crowd parted as a group of horsemen cantered out of the city. Na pulled himself close to a ditch beside the road to watch them go by. In the centre of the party was a mandarin in silk robes surrounded by attendants and guards. To one side, slightly behind the mandarin, was a young boy who rode close to the ditch where he sat. The boy reined his horse in to look more closely at the beggar in the ditch. Na averted his eyes lest he offend this powerful group, but the boy continued to stare and finally said, 'Look at me, let me see your face'.

Na raised his head and looked into the face of his beloved brother Ch'eng.

The two brothers rose to greet each other with outstretched arms. They held onto each other as though one might disappear again, Na's tears staining his brother's embroidered silks.

Those at the rear of the mandarin's party had reined in their horses to watch this unlikely reunion. One of the attendants then rode forward to tell the mandarin, who ordered the attendant to give his horse to the stranger. Na rode with the wealthy procession which led him to the mandarin's house.

Eager to hear how his brother had fared, Na didn't even wait to eat or wash. Ch'eng told him how the tiger had dropped him at the roadside where he had lain unconscious all night. Early the next morning the mandarin had passed by and observed that Ch'eng did not have the appearance of a peasant or beggar. The mandarin took the boy home and cared for him until he had recovered although his memory of the past was clouded. Ch'eng was an honest and dutiful boy and having no son of his own, the mandarin adopted him.

While they were talking the servants had gathered clothes from the inner rooms and poured out bowls of water so that Na could wash. In the evening Na was called to the mandarin's table to share a meal. Na told him of his family, his village and his travels but the mandarin wanted to hear more details of Na's father.

'He is a Shantung man from the T'ung-ch'ang district.'

'How strange, he is from the same place as me,' replied the mandarin. 'Why did he leave for Honan?'

'His wife was abducted by soldiers when they were married and everything he had was taken. He had business contacts in Honan and established a new life there.'

The mandarin proceeded to ask questions about Na's father's family names and background. He listened intently to every reply but said nothing. Finally, he had heard enough and left the room. When he returned, he was accompanied by a frail old woman. The company in the room stood to bow to her while she sat close to Na.

'Are you Chang Ping-chih's grandson?'

When Na acknowledged that he was, the old lady burst into tears and turned to her son, the mandarin:

'Meet your younger brothers Na and Ch'eng. Three years after my marriage I was abducted to be a slave in a mandarin's family. Just six months afterwards you were born, and six months later the mandarin died. You were accepted as his heir and appointed mandarin. I tried to find out what happened to my husband but there were no answers. How could I know he was so far away?'

When their stories had been revealed there were so many reasons to celebrate. Musicians were called for and the servants prepared aromatic dishes for a party that went late into the night.

The reunited brothers made a promise that they would return to Honan and settle down there. The mandarin would resign his post and, with the wealth that he had accumulated, would buy a family estate. Only old Mrs. Chang was hesitant.

'Will my husband accept me after all these years? He may turn me away.'

The mandarin would not allow her to speak further.

'We are a family. How can there be a place where parents are not valued. We will return together.'

And so it was that the family sold their house and travelled with their retinue to Honan. Ch'eng was the first to enter his father's house in Honan. He found him bent over a table in the courtyard and bowed down before him. The old man felt a surge of joy – his wife had died and he believed his sons had gone forever, now they waited to greet him. His sons entered, followed by the wife who had been torn from him. The long separated husband and wife, both in tears, held each other for a long time. As they embraced the whole courtyard became filled up with servants, horses, travelling chests, carpet bags and precious belongings.

The following week, Mr. Chang found a grand house for the family with a spacious apartment for each member. Tutors were employed for Na and Ch'eng, the rooms were filled with fine objects, the storehouses were stocked, servants were busy in the halls and the stables were full of fine horses.

The Emperor of Literature

The god of literature, venerated by Confucians and others alike, is also known as the Emperor of Literature. His titles are Wen Chang Ti Kun, Wen Chang or just Wen Ti. The focus of scholars' devotion is Kung Fu Tzu himself, but the legends of Wen Chang place him well before the sage was born, well before the 5th century BC. For Wen Chang is a god who comes to earth to bring wisdom and understanding to the people. According to the legends and accounts, he has come to earth seventeen times in different human forms. Wen Chang himself is a constellation of six stars in attendance upon the Great Bear. When Wen Chang perceives that learning and wisdom is weak upon the earth, he descends and takes human form.

One of his earliest appearances was some three thousand years ago, in the long gone kingdom of Shu, in what is today Szechwan.

The kingdom of Shu was surrounded by neighbouring kingdoms who all wished to take over its rich lands and fertile hills. Of these, the most expansionist and the most envious was ruled by the Lord of Chin. For years he had cast around for ways to capture the kingdom of Shu, but the armies and peoples of Shu were vigilant and prepared to fight to the death for their lands.

Still the Lord of Chin would not rest. He sought advice from the wise men of his court. One of them, known for his cunning, gave them this advice,

'My Lord, the King of Shu has a young son. He has just now come of marriageable age. What if your own dear daughter were sent to him as a bride? The people of Shu would take this as a sign of peace; as a sign that you were content to let things be; as a sign that they need not be vigilant concerning us.'

The Lord of Chin frowned and interrupted the courtier. 'But what do I gain by giving such an impression and by sending my daughter into such a position. It will look as if I am the weak one.'

'My Lord,' replied the cunning courtier, 'when you have lulled the people and the king into thinking there is nothing to be frightened of, that is when you strike. And you will be able to strike for your daughter will have to take with her a retinue of strong servants and perhaps her own guards! Therefore, in the very heart of the country, at the very centre of the kingdom, you will have your own men. When the time is ripe, you advance from our borders and they will fling open the city gates. Victory will be ours, and all this before the people of Shu even know you have become their enemy again!'

The Lord of Chin liked this plan. He liked it very much and immediately sent off ambassadors to Shu, offering the hand of his daughter to the young prince of Shu. He couched his letters in such a way as to make it sound as if he was seeking eternal friendship.

In the Kingdom of Shu, the ambassadors and their offer were received with great rejoicing. At last it seemed as if the old enemy had accepted that Shu should be left in peace.

All seemed to be going the way of the evil schemes of Chin, when Wen Chang manifested himself to save the kingdom from such deceit. Just as the marriage was about to be performed, and the daughter of the Lord of Chin was in her rooms preparing, Wen Chang appeared. But he was not in the guise of a human being. His form was that of a giant snake, terrible of appearance, terrifying in size. The daughter shrieked with horror and ran from the palace. Wen Chang drove her and her retinue out into the countryside. Then he lifted up a mountain and brought it down upon them all, crushing them to death beneath it. The mountain, called Tzu Ku, in the area of Tzu Tung in Szechwan, is there to this day and atop it is the temple to Wen Chang in his form as the Thunder God who manifested himself as the snake to save the kingdom of Shu.

Wen Chang also manifested himself as Chang Ya Tzu, known as the Spirit of Tzu Tung – the mountain region mentioned above. He appeared as Chang Ya Tzu around 300 AD and died after a violent fight, defending the Office of which he was in charge.

At other times he was revealed as a wise and just official who became the President of the Board of Ceremonies, and who was renowned for his wisdom and astuteness. For this manifestation he took the name Chang Ya and was born during the Tang dynasty (618 – 907 AD). It was after this incarnation that he was given the Celestial Office of Keeper of the Registers of Titles. The Jade Emperor commissioned him to look out for those who were worthy of award and to bestow titles and honours upon those students and officials who deserved them. To him also falls responsibility for punishing those who betray their posts or offices and exploit the people.

One of his most dramatic interventions was in the year 1000 AD. He yet again appeared in Szechwan, this time at the capital of the province, Chengdu. At that time the rebel Wang Chun had seized the city and was using it as the base for his revolt against the Sung dynasty. Emperor Hsien Ping sent his loyal and devout general, Lei Yu Chung to retake the city. But try as they would, it held out against them and Wang Chun mocked their efforts. In an attempt to break their morale, General Lei Yu Chung fired arrows into the beleaguered town, carrying messages offering an amnesty to any who surrendered.

However, despite this early attempt at propaganda, the rebels stood firm and it seemed as if nothing would shift them.

Then, suddenly and from nowhere, a man appeared who mounted a ladder and, gesticulating towards the rebels, shouted in a loud voice that he came bearing a message. He claimed that the spirit of Tzu Tung (Wen Chang) had commanded him to say that the rebel city would fall into the hands of the Emperor's army on the twentieth day of the ninth month and that no-one would escape from the city alive.

The rebel troops, hearing this proclamation, tried their hardest to bring down the prophet with arrows, but to no avail. Seeming to be protected from all that could be flung against him, the speaker continued to denounce the rebels and then disappeared as suddenly as he had appeared.

Sure enough, on the twentieth day of the ninth month General Lei attacked Chengdu and the city fell. Not a single rebel soldier escaped alive. To commemorate this event, the General repaired the temple of Tzu Tung, originally built after his miraculous intervention to save the old kingdom of Shu.

Wen Chang is not alone in his Office as Bestower of Titles, Scholar Deity and Emperor of Literature. In particular he has one very special colleague who usually stands either before or beside him. And he is a most odd looking gentleman. He too comes from a constellation of stars in the Great Bear, the four which make up the chariot of the Great Bear and thus he is to be found in the same part of the Heavens as the Wen Chang constellation.

The name of this deity constellation is Kuei Hsing and the story told of him is a very special one, as indeed is the form of his statue. Kuei Hsing is usually depicted standing upon the head of a sea monster. Kuei Hsing's left leg is raised behind him as if he is running. In his right hand he holds a writing brush. In his left, a seal of office. What is most striking, however, is his hideous face.

Long ago a son was born to a poor family in China. He was much loved by his family but he was hideously ugly. No matter how you looked at him, he was grotesque. But he was of delightful demeanour and exceptionally bright. The family, poor as they were, recognized that in his wisdom and knowledge they had a gem which if polished and perfected would bring honour and fortune to the whole family.

For years this child, Chung Kuei, studied. Night and day he learned to master the Classics of Kung Fu Tzu. Year after year he took his exams and progressed rapidly, rising from town to city to county then to provincial examinations. At last he reached the peak, the apex of the Imperial examination world. Travelling to the Imperial City, he entered the Imperial examinations. To no one's great surprise, he came first, clearly the best of a good group that year. An outstanding scholar, even if his visage was a terrible one.

It was the practice of the Emperor personally to meet the top scholar and to present him with a golden rose in commemoration of his success. Chung Kuei duly turned up at the Imperial Palace, and was eagerly admitted to the Imperial Presence. However, disaster struck. The Emperor, seeing Chung Kuei's terrible appearance took fright and refused to have the scholar in his presence.

Chung Kuei, crushed and humiliated by this, rushed from the Imperial Palace and, running to the sea, cast himself upon it, intent upon committing suicide. The gods, seeing this injustice, sent a giant fish or sea monster to rescue him. At the very moment when he was about to go under for the last time, Chung Kuei found himself being lifted up on the head of the creature. But he was not just rescued from the sea. The creature continued to rise, up through the clouds. Up into the sky; up into the very firmaments themselves. The fish bore him to the Keui Constellation and there the gods gave him command over the fortunes of scholars. From there, along with his brother in Scholarship Wen Chang, Kuei Hsing looks after the fortunes of the scholars and of officials.

Wen Chang is accompanied by another god, Chu I, Red Gown as he is commonly known. A story will illustrate the role Red Gown plays in this world of Exams and Scholars.

Long ago in the Tang dynasty (618 – 907) there was a young, earnest and intelligent scholar called Lu Chi whose physiognomy showed to those who could see that he could become an immortal. The Heavenly Princess Tai Yin saw this young man, realized his potential and desired to marry him. After much activity, a meeting in Heaven was arranged between the Princess and Lu Chi. Standing before the lovely Princess, Lu Chi was offered three different possible futures. The first was to marry the Princess, live in her Heavenly Palace and be an immortal. The second choice was to return to earth and to live as an immortal upon earth. The third choice was to return to earth and to rise to a position of great authority and thus to help the people.

At first Lu Chi, somewhat overcome by all that was happening to him and much taken with the beauty of the Princess, decided to marry her and to remain in Heaven. The Princess was overjoyed and the Emperor of Heaven was duly informed. The Emperor of Heaven, however, felt that Lu Chi should be given time to consider his decision. Shortly afterwards the Emperor sent a Divine Messenger, Chu I, to interview the young man.

Chu I asked the young scholar, did he wish to stay in Heaven? Lu Chi did not answer, for he was torn by doubts now. The Princess begged him and asked Chu I to wait and try again. Sure enough, Chu I asked a second time, 'Do you wish to stay here in Heaven and become an immortal?'

Lu Chi looked up. He had made up his mind. 'I have dedicated my life to study because I wish to serve the people and to become a Minister in the Imperial Court.'

On hearing this, Chu I ordered that Lu Chi be taken back to earth.

Upon his return, he applied himself even more diligently than before to his studies. In due course he took the Imperial Exam and was placed highest. Over the years his noble service drew him to the attention of the Emperor and he rose to become a Minister. On the day that he was due to die, his face changed. His head became that of a panther, his lips those of a dragon and his colouring was that of an immortal – blue. Witnessed by many, his body rose from the earth and ascended into Heaven.

The story of Su Wu

In the days of the Han dynasty, Emperor Wu reigned from 141 – 87 BC. A mighty warrior himself, he drew to his service men of great talent. Amongst these were two outstanding officials, Su Wu and

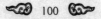

Li Ling. Both were able, talented, scholarly and steeped in the traditions of China. To the north west of the Empire were a ferocious warrior tribe known as the Hsiung-nu. Against these people Emperor Wu directed his best armies but with little effect. In the course of these actions, Li Ling was captured and held prisoner by the Hsiung-nu.

Eventually the Emperor decided to try diplomacy and he chose Su Wu to head the embassy to the Hsiung-nu, to request peace and the release of Li Ling. The embassy travelled across inhospitable terrain until at last they reached the camp of the Hsiung-nu army and people. Here they were seized and manhandled. Offered the choice of death or of changing their loyalty to serve the Hsiung-nu, Su Wu stood firm and resolute, honourable to the last. To his horror he discovered that Li Ling, offered the same choice, had caved in and had joined the Hsiung-nu.

To try and break Su Wu, the Hsiung-nu threw him into a pit and left him to starve to death. Each day they returned to ask if he had changed his mind. Each day he restated his loyalty to the Emperor of China. The pit was a deep hole out in the countryside. Here Su Wu was kept for days without any food or drink. Occasionally it snowed and he took succour from eating the snow. Seeing his determination and in part admiring him for this, the Hsiung-nu sent him afar off to the farthest west of their empire, far, far away from China and any hope of rescue. Here for nineteen years he guarded sheep, becoming in the process a skilled shepherd. Every so often the Hsiung-nu would renew their offer of release, of honours and glory, if only he would renounce his loyalty to the Emperor and enter their service.

At last, nineteen years after being taken prisoner, the Hsiung-nu, recognizing him to be a man of unquestionable honour, released him and he was at last able to return home.

The traitor Li Ling never came home.

4

Taoist

Ti Kuai Li's Temptation

Ti Kuai Li found peace in his mountain cave far from the gossip and business of village life. He had wood to build a fire, slept on a straw mattress and grew enough vegetables to provide a simple evening meal. He collected water from a mountain stream and grew rice on the small terraces lower down the mountain. Once the day's routine had been completed he sat down to study the Taoist scriptures, and when storms broke out or a bitter wind pierced the cave entrance he was so engrossed he hardly noticed.

One spring morning as Ti Kuai Li was planting seeds outside the cave he was approached by a woodcutter he had never seen before. He beckoned to a stone seat and offered the stranger tea and a bowl of rice. The stranger revealed many strange things, he spoke of magicians and spirits that appeared in the night, and of hungry ghosts and devils who plagued the wicked.

Ti Kuai Li listened until the man had finished his story. There was a silence between them and then the woodcutter spoke:

'You will have a long life and be a learned scholar. Your wisdom and compassion will be recognized and you will be a source of comfort and happiness to those in need. One day you will become an Immortal and rise from this ocean of bitter troubles.'

'How can I ever hope to attain this wisdom,' replied Ti Kuai Li. 'It is a hard path and one that few can follow. I have never searched for immortality but I want to understand the Tao and I am willing to study hard.'

The woodcutter seemed pleased with Ti Kuai Li's response but did not comment further. When he next spoke it was to ask a favour.

'I am not wise in the ways of nature and the spirits although I have heard many stories, but I have a daughter who is devoted to me and wants me to live a long and healthy life. In order to grant me blessings she wants to study with a wise teacher. Will you be her teacher?'

'I cannot do that. How can I be a teacher when I have so much to learn myself?'

'What you say could be true,' replied the old man. He then thanked the woodcutter for his kindness and left.

Three days later, as the sun began to disappear behind the mountain, the woodcutter approached the cave again. In the dim light Ti Kuai Li could see a beautiful girl standing a short distance from the cave.

'This is my only daughter. She is a devoted girl and ever since I told her about you she has insisted on being your student. I have informed her that you do not want a student but she refuses to eat until you become her teacher. I have no choice but to bring her to you, so please grant her wish and become her master.'

Ti Kuai Li averted his eyes from the girl but it was too late to object again for the woodcutter hurriedly left them with a command to his daughter to obey Ti Kuai Li's orders.

The girl's eyes were fixed on the floor as she slowly approached Ti Kuai Li and knelt at his feet. Ti Kuai Li turned in embarrassment and went into the cave. He sat in the corner of the cave by the fire and picked up his Taoist scriptures still uncomfortable with the girl's presence. She followed him into the cave and began to stir the pot of vegetables boiling over the fire. She then picked up a broom and swept the dust towards the cave entrance, from time to time sneaking a glance at Ti Kuai Li's handsome face. When the cleaning was finished she cautiously approached her teacher.

'Master, I do not want to disturb your studies, I know how important they are to you but surely life is lonely here. Don't you want to have the company of a wife and a family to take care of you in your old age?'

Ti Kuai Li did not look up from his books.

'Surely, you become lonely here with nothing but insects, rabbits and birds for company. Tell me what you are thinking, no one else can hear, it is just the two of us and whatever you say will be safe with me.'

Ti Kuai Li put his book down and walked to the entrance of the cave but the girl would not be defeated.

'You must hear my story. I don't really want to be a student but I have to escape from my father. I have told him I wanted to be a nun to escape the marriage he has arranged for me. My future husband is an ugly man, he has heavy, long dark eyebrows, enormous ears and one is pierced to carry a heavy brass ring. He walks with a limp and his body is twisted and hairy. I would rather spend my life in study than marry such a man. By studying with you I am obeying my father and avoiding marriage. But you are a handsome man and if you took me for a wife both my problems would be solved at once.'

Ti Kuai Li still did not respond. And the girl continued to praise his looks and his wisdom. She told him what a fine housewife she would make and how he would want for nothing. She painted a picture of a warm and clean house where she and their family would be waiting for him in the evening, obedient to his every wish. And Ti Kuai Li still stood silent, looking out towards the mountain.

Two hours passed and the girl finally fell asleep by the fire, exhausted from her efforts. Ti Kuai Li listened for the steady rhythm of her breathing and in the certainty that she was asleep he pulled his mattress to a corner of the cave, far from the girl. The temperature dropped during the night, a storm rumbled overhead and sheets of rain slanted through the cave entrance.

The girl woke with a start as a roll of thunder passed overhead and in the darkness she could make out the shape of Ti Kuai Li. She crept over silently and huddled close to him. Ti Kuai Li woke with a start.

'What are you doing? Go away, leave me.'

But she moved even closer, shivering in her thin cotton dress.

'Put your arms around me, I'm so cold and you can protect me.'

Ti Kuai Li withdrew further into the damp corner of the cave and the girl followed him, whispering gently to him, persuading him to hold her, to take her as his wife. Ti Kuai Li steadfastly refused, not daring to even look at the girl. The more soft and gently she cajoled him, the more determined he was not to succumb.

In the morning, the woodcutter arrived as Ti Kuai Li was washing pots outside the cave.

'Where is my daughter?' he demanded.

'I cannot tell you. She suddenly left in the night.'

'Did you harm her? You must have done something to make her go. Did you rape her?'

Ti Kuai Li calmed the woodcutter.

'I did not touch your daughter and she came to no harm. I did not hurt her in any way, I would never do such a thing.'

The woodcutter smiled and he held Ti Kuai Li gently by the arm. 'I believe what you say. I know that you are a man of honour with a deep understanding of Taoism. We are similar in nature.'

Ti Kuai Li heard a noise in the undergrowth and turned in that direction. When he turned again to face the woodcutter he had gone and in front of him stood a man in a long blue robe. Ti Kuai Li recognized him as the great sage, Lao Tzu. A piece of wood lay in his outstretched hand.

'I fashioned the girl from this piece of wood to tempt you but you did not succumb. You are a man of strong character and not easily fooled by trickery.'

Lao Tzu searched in the leather bag hanging from his belt, pulled out a small white tablet and gave it to Ti Kuai Li.

'Swallow this tablet.'

Ti Kuai Li did as he had been told. Lao Tzu then turned and began his descent down the hill. Ti Kuai Li swallowed the tablet. He felt a surge of energy and from that moment onwards he was never tired nor ill, never thirsty nor hungry. He journeyed throughout the countryside helping the destitute and defending their causes. Every few months he would return to the privacy of his cave to meditate and study the Taoist scriptures.

Ti Kuai Li is given the gift of flight

One afternoon, as Ti Kuai Li sat outside his cave, he noticed two men cautiously approach a wooden hut at the edge of the forest. They opened the door, forced one of the floor boards with an axe and hid two heavy sackcloth bags under the floor. They nervously glanced around at the doorway to check that no one had seen them and ran back down the hill.

Ti Kuai Li watched everything that happened but did nothing. Several days later when he was visiting a tea house in a local town, he was approached by an elderly man with a white beard.

'Do you mind if I join you?' he asked, but without waiting for a reply he sat down next to him. As Ti Kuai Li sipped his tea he was aware that this stranger was looking at him intently.

Eventually the old man spoke, 'I can tell by looking at your face that you will become very wealthy.'

'Your words could come true for I know where two bags of money are hidden.'

Ti Kuai Li recounted what he had seen earlier in the week and the old man urged him to take advantage of his good luck.

'What does it matter if you keep it because it is stolen anyway, no one will blame you. Without money you will be bitter and unhappy.'

But no amount of urging would persuade Ti Kuai Li to take the money. He only shrugged each time the old man reminded him of the wonderful things he could own. Why did he need wealth? What would he do with all those possessions? Ti Kuai Li was content with what he had.

Two nights later Ti Kuai Li met the old man again in the dark precincts of a temple. This time the old man brought out a small tablet from a pigskin bag hanging from his belt.

'Swallow this,' he said. Ti Kuai Li sensed that he could trust this stranger and did as he was told.

As soon as he had swallowed the pill Ti Kuai Li felt a weight-less feeling inside his body. He began to walk out of the temple, but instead of moving at his normal speed he found himself trav-elling faster than a swallow, through the dark lanes of the town. The houses ended and the fields passed by faster and faster, then he looked down and realized that his feet were not touching the earth. He flew higher and higher and rose above the fields and walled towns, above forests and mountains.

The old man had not been a fortune-teller, he was the sage Lao Tzu. Once again the great Immortal had come to help and teach him.

Ti Kuai Li is given the Elixir of Immortality

Ti Kuai Li used the precious gifts that Lao Tzu had given him to help the poor and to spread Taoist teachings. He could fly faster than the swiftest bird and no illness could harm his body. He was well-known and respected as a learned man and at Lao Tzu's request he accepted a young student, Li Ching.

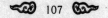

One day Ti Kuai Li told his student that he had to travel to Wah Shan mountain to visit Lao Tzu.

'But how can you travel such a great distance? It is thousands of miles from here and will take months to walk there.'

'Do not ask any more questions,' answered Ti Kuai Li. 'My body will remain with you but my soul will fly to the mountain. If I do not return by the end of the seventh day I will have become immortal and you can burn my body.'

As Ti Kuai Li sat still and meditated, a plume of smoke appeared above his head. Li Chang placed his finger below his master's nose to feel his breath but it had gone. The young student waited by his master's body for six days refusing to move but on the morning of the seventh day a messenger arrived with urgent news.

'Your mother is dangerously ill and wants to see you before she dies, you must come with me.'

Li Chang felt that he had no choice, he must be with his mother. It was the seventh day and since Ti Kuai Li had not returned, the student burnt his body.

Li Chang had not travelled far from the cave when he saw a beggar dying by the roadside. He knelt at the man's side to see if he could help to ease his pain but there was nothing he could do. The dying man's clothes were ragged, his hair was short, his eyebrows long and untidy. He wore a heavy brass ring in one ear and a pan lid on his head. One leg was thin and disfigured and a broken wooden crutch was thrown to one side. The beggar died while Li Chang was at his side but in his rush to see his mother he had no time to bury him.

Li Chang had just descended the mountain when Ti Kuai Li's soul appeared back at the cave. He hovered above the earth where he had left his body but it was gone. Perhaps Li Chang had moved his body and so he searched the cave and the surrounding plot of land but it had disappeared. In dismay, Ti Kuai Li realized that the pile of smouldering ashes was all that remained of his previous form. Time was running out and unless he entered the body of someone who had recently died he could no longer be immortal. He looked around and saw the deformed beggar and so he reluctantly entered his body.

When Ti Kuai Li pulled himself to the ground in his new form, he heard someone laughing behind him. He turned to see a wizened man carrying a bag of herbs and potions.

'Do you know me?' enquired Ti Kuai Li.

'I know you well. Come to me and I will help you. This bottle contains a magic elixir which can ease pain and heal wounds. Your body is disfigured and people will be frightened when they see you but you will have the gift of healing. The poor will call you to their homes and the rich will summon you to their estates. People will beg you to come to them.'

'How much medicine does this bottle hold?' asked Ti Kuai Li.

'This medicine will last forever; as long as people are sick there will be medicine in the bottle.'

The herbalist tipped the bottle and spread metal powder into the palm of his hand. He then uncorked the gourd at his side, poured water onto the powder and mixed it to a paste. He skilfully moulded the paste to form a long metal rod.

'This crutch will never rust or break, it will be your support wherever you go.'

The herbalist handed Ti Kuai Li the bottle and the crutch.

'From this day on you will join the immortals but I must leave you now.'

'Wait,' cried Ti Kuai Li, still in a state of shock.

'I cannot wait,' replied the old man. 'I must return to Lao Tzu. I am merely his messenger.'

The herbalist left and as Ti Kuai Li watched him walk slowly away from the cave he realized that he had just been in the presence of Lao Tzu. From that day on Ti Kuai Li travelled in the form of a beggar through many lands, healing the sick and defending the poor.

The Immortal's Dream

Han Chung Li had stayed in the ancient imperial city of Chang-An for fourteen days. Dressed as a general he had been lavishly entertained by the local governors and officials – he had discussed the affairs of state, heard of the local intrigue and learnt of the petty squabbles. He had taken enough of city life and left on foot for a long journey to wherever the road took him. Half a day's walk from the city walls he stopped by an inn, frequented by officials making the journey to and from the capital. As always, he found a corner seat outside the inn and sat back to watch the preoccupied officials pursue their affairs.

That afternoon Lu Tung Pin was travelling along the same road, he wore the look of a man with many details to consider and officials to answer to. In those days he had yet to become an immortal and had ambitious dreams of high rank in the government. For generations his family had been high-ranking officials, serving their superiors with a respect inherited from father to son. They also delegated wisely and their family achievements were well recognized – they wore the feather of office in their hat and fine silk gowns emblazoned with their insignia of office. Lu Tung Pin continued this honourable tradition and had brought great honour to his family by achieving high marks in the imperial exams. There seemed little that would stop his rise to power.

Han Chung Li sipped his warm rice wine as Lu Tung Pin's escort drew up to the inn. They beat on their drums to announce the arrival of this important man. But Lu Tung Pin was more than an efficient servant of the state, his studies in law and administration were matched by his studies in poetry and philosophy. He immersed himself in the wisdom of the immortals and often reflected on the words of sages and the way of Heaven. But in the end his public life had to take precedence if he hoped to achieve the feather of office.

Like the other officials entering the inn that day Lu Tung Pin was preoccupied with his affairs and his duties. But there was something about him that caught the attention of the wise immortal. He could see into the soul of an individual in a way that someone caught in the cycle of human life could not. He beckoned Lu Tung Pin to his table and Han Chung Li obliged the general who had offered to share his table.

Over a jug of wine the two discussed the business of the day, the entertainment of city life, the condition of the crops. It was an easy, affable conversation. Without their realizing, dusk had closed in and they continued to talk while the tables filled up with the evening guests and the horses in the stable had their feed and settled for the night. They spoke of their ancestors, of immortality and of the Tao, and Lu Tung Pin discovered that he had many questions to ask. It was a long time since he had sat with a wise man and did not know when the opportunity would come again so he stayed until the smoke from the fire and the wine made him drowsy. He attempted to stand but could not, he fell back into his chair, head to one side and was fast asleep.

He had a strange and startling dream; he wanted to pull himself out of it and be in control of his life again but the dream had hold of him. He saw himself travelling away from the imperial city where he had gained the favour of the emperor and now he wore a feather of office. He administered wisely and after two years was promoted to a senior post in the Emperor's court. The years passed quickly in his dream, favours were heaped on him and his family. He honoured the gods and his ancestors, he was respected at court and he was known in the highest offices of government. Lesser officials were in awe of his power and his anger and when important state decisions were made he was consulted.

Lu Tung Pin's rise to power had also cultivated jealous enemies and even the Emperor became tired of seeing his face in court.

One day Lu Tung Pin offended him and he was dismissed. His enemies soon closed in telling the Emperor alarming tales about Lu Tung Pin's bad judgement, his secretive negotiations and his ambitions to power. Lu Tung Pin was summoned before the Emperor and, witnessed by the assembled court, was sent into exile. Shame had been heaped on his family but worse was to come. The Emperor ordered the execution of his family, their house was stripped of its goods and their ancestral hall was left to decay.

Beyond the borders of the state Lu Tung Pin was left to mourn. Anonymous and stripped of rank he wandered unknown villages and one night in the quiet countryside he sat by the road and wept. Suddenly he awoke, startled to find himself still at the inn with the wise stranger sitting next to him.

The next morning Lu Tung Pin did not arrive in the imperial capital to meet the civil servants waiting for him. He said goodbye to his servants, bridled his horse and followed Han Chung Li. He realized that the way of power was not the true Way and so he cast aside all the trappings of a high official. The two men travelled to the Ho Ling Mountains where Lu Tung Pin served, trained, and studied alongside Han Chung Li, as he learnt the divine mysteries of immortality from his master. Years passed and eventually Lu Tung Pin himself became an immortal.

Lu Tung Pin's Revenge

The Eight Immortals were wise but they were not perfect. They knew the secrets of alchemy, they understood the ways of Heaven, they could change shape at will or fly to the clouds. But they could be cross and argumentative, they preferred comfortable seats and good wine and they could be easily insulted.

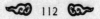

When it came to holding their temper or swallowing their pride, Lu Tung Pin was the weakest. He was young, exuberant and boastful and although he tried to set a good example, he was a bad loser.

One summer, Lu Tung Pin decided to take a journey down the Ou River. He was allowed passage on a small trading boat that stopped regularly to pick up rice or to put off pigs and chickens. As they sailed the calm waters in between villages Lu Tung Pin and the helmsman would play chess. The helmsman moved slowly and deliberately, thinking through his moves and keeping a watchful eye on his opponent. Lu Tung Pin was more hasty, moving his pieces quickly and impatiently so that he could win. But he didn't win and with each defeat his anger increased. On the fifth day of their journey, after losing again, Lu Tung Pin hurled the chess set across the water. His immortal force was so great the chess set took root on the banks of the Ou river and from that time on there was a mountain shaped like a chess set.

Lu Tung Pin was still not satisfied, he remembered his humiliation in the winter months and kept the secret to himself. Had they known, the other immortals would have calmed him down but nevertheless they would have found it amusing, perhaps offering to have a game or two of chess with him.

Spring arrived and Lu Tung Pin made arrangements to spend summer back on the Ou River, his mind set on revenge. By now his resentment had magnified – it was not just the helmsman who had offended him, all the inhabitants of the Ou river were to blame.

He arrived in disguise at the banks of the Ou river and filled two large sacks with earth. He tied them at either end of an iron pole, slung them across his shoulders and set off to block the flow of the river. Using his magic powers he could make the bags expand to become huge grey boulders which no team of harnessed oxen could shift. As he took off his shoes to wade into the water he was stopped by an old farmer.

'Stranger, come quickly, I need your help,' said the old man, clutching his arm. 'My pig has escaped but my legs are weak and I cannot catch him. Will you bring him back to me?'

Lu Tung Pin lifted the iron pole off his shoulders and laid the bags on the riverside. The pig had disappeared into distant farm buildings and Lu Tung Pin followed in his direction. The old farmer waited until he was out of sight and then swapped the sturdy iron pole for a dark wooden pole. Lu Tung Pin came back into view with a squealing and unwilling pig wrapped in his arms. The old farmer tethered the pig to a gatepost, thanked Lu Tung Pin and bade him goodbye.

Lu Tung Pin swung the pole back on his shoulder but within seconds there was a resounding crack as the weight of the bags twisted and snapped the wood. The bags thumped to the floor and started to roll, spitting out soil as they gained speed. When they finally came to rest there was a mound of soil big enough to hide a field of sweet potatoes. The accident brought his anger to the boil and he set to a new plan of vengeance.

His target was the widest part of the Ou river, it would be the scene of his perfect revenge. He lifted a magic duster from his pigskin bag and waved it above a heap of discarded earthenware wine jugs in a nearby hollow. He commanded lightning to flash across the jars and a piercing white light broke from the clouds onto the field. The jars disappeared and in their place was a flock of bewildered white sheep. At the command of 'Change', the duster became a sturdy willow stick and Lu Tung Pin gathered the sheep and drove them along the willow bank. He herded them towards a small hamlet of wooden houses clustered around a shallow river crossing. Lu Tung Pin made his way over the flat, slippery stepping stones and the sheep attempted to follow. Their hooves could not grip, they staggered on the moss and slipped onto the pebbled floor of the river. The first of the bedraggled sheep made it to the far side while Lu Tung Pin watched and waited for them.

As he sat there a woodcutter approached the far side of the river. He wanted to cross but the sheep were still floundering and dusk was beginning to fall. 'Could you part your sheep so I can make my way home?' he called out. Lu Tung Pin waded over to the man clearing a path amongst the sheep. The woodcutter nodded his thanks and stepped out onto the stone but halfway across his way was blocked by a lame sheep. Unexpectedly, the bundle of wood thrown across his shoulder became unbearably heavy, his back doubled and his knees began to give way. It was as though someone had placed two huge stones on his shoulders. His voice rose in the dark, 'Help me, my back is breaking.'

But the only response from Lu Tung Pin was a mischievous smile and the woodcutter knew he had been tricked. To save himself the woodcutter hit the sheep in front of him. The sheep slipped and tumbled into the stream but at the touch of water on its wool the sheep changed back into an earthenware jar. Lu Tung Pin was furious, he leapt to his feet and scrambled across the water to the young man, 'You clumsy fool, you've killed one of my flock, I'll make you pay for this.'

But the woodcutter was not easily tricked. He picked up a broken shard from the water, 'Look, it's only an earthenware jar, what is this worth, less than a spoon of rice? Whatever evil you're practising will stop here or I'll make a report to the town judge.'

Lu Tung Pin was anxious not to draw attention to himself. Creating trouble amongst the humans could cause untold damage and so he adopted a more conciliatory tone.

'Why are we arguing, it's so unnecessary when we can talk instead. I am going to tell you a secret but you must not repeat this to another living being. I am the immortal Lu Tung Pin, no doubt you fear the magic I can create with the movement of my arm or a word from my lips. My power is greater than your imagination can dream of. These sheep are earthenware pots, at my command they will change and multiply, there will be a mountain of pots. I'm on my way to block the river so that the lowlands of either side will be flooded. Go now, run from the flood.'

But the woodcutter's only thought was for his friends along the river and the innocent people of the villages. He said nothing to Lu Tung Pin but nodded as though in approval. Once the wood-cutter was safely across the remaining crossing stones he yelled out, breaking the calm of dusk:

'Out, get out of your houses. Move quickly or you may die. Save yourselves now or you will be killed.' The doors of the houses were flung open and the rich light from the lamps and fires came pouring out. Raised voices travelled through the evening air as the villagers ran from their houses brandishing rakes, hoes, scythes and saws. Chickens and ducks fled in their path and the village dogs followed on yelping and barking, infected by this sudden commotion. The sheep dispersed in fear, running in all directions, tripping over each other in the chaos. A few huddled below an overhang in the river bank but none could escape the onslaught. Every sheep struck down turned into an earthenware pot and no-one could find a safe refuge.

Before Lu Tung Pin could escape the woodcutter had cornered him. Wielding a wooden staff he lunged at the Immortal, and caught him with a sharp blow to the leg. Lu Tung Pin crouched with the pain then hobbled away into the night. He tried to use his magic powers and fly far away from the scene but Heaven was watching, he had to take his punishment. It would be a long time before Lu Tung Pin would dare return.

That night, the villagers gathered the earthenware jars scattered across their lands and along the riverbank. They loaded them onto carts and tipped them into a nearby lake but there was still the sediment from wine in the bottom of the jars. Over the years the sediment seeped into the deep waters of the lake and in the evening as the villagers walked by the lake they could smell wine. To this day it is known as 'Wine Lake'.

The House with the Alabaster Door

Each Immortal travelled the mountains and the plains of China and beyond. They often travelled in disguise, talking to villagers, observing the peasants, beggars, landowners, traders, sages and disciples. No story was ever forgotten, they were stored up to be retold at the Immortals' bridge.

The eight Immortals met regularly at the bridge, it was their private time and no human could hear or see what happened. But these meetings weren't usually marked out by feats of magic, they were relaxing times – a chance to gossip, play cards or entertain each other with stories of their travels.

One particular afternoon, the eight were gathered on the small, stone-arched bridge singing songs in the bright, afternoon sunshine. As the sun sank lower they called for a story, something to entertain them in the evening. Chang Kuo Lao stood up and addressed the attentive Immortals with news of a dispute in a distant province.

'A day's walk from Man Yo Street, there is a house surrounded by tall fir trees and in its main entrance is a finely carved alabaster door. The master of the house is K'uang Tzu Lien, a wealthy merchant and farmer. He owns ten thousand fertile fields, his clothes are sewn from the finest silk and in every room is an ivory chest encrusted with gold and silver. It would take twenty strong men just to carry these chests, but his wealth has been accumulated at the expense of the poor. The peasants who work on his land are poorly fed and the labourers who build his houses are underpaid. I have heard that he will be sixty years old in a few days and plans to hold a party, even now the servants are working from before dawn preparing the banquet. In order to prove that he is the most powerful man in the area he has filled the holes in the road with rice and laid a fine red woollen carpet over the rice to smooth the way.'

The eight Immortals who had encountered so much poverty on their journeys through the provinces were enraged at this waste. Ti Kuai Li stood up:

'How dare he waste food and wool as though it were dirt to walk on when the peasants have so little they can barely survive. I will teach him a lesson that will not be forgotten by him or by the generations of the family that follow him.'

As he stood up from his place on the bridge the gourd hanging at his side changed to a begging bowl. Using his magical powers of flight he rose from the ground and within a few seconds had arrived at K'uang Tzu Lien's house. Layers of finely carved, brightly painted wooden beams formed a roof above the house and at the corner of each beam a golden painted dragon rose into the air. The most skilled craftsmen from the area had carved the stone into an array of animals and worked the wood into the most intricate shapes. The door had been fashioned in one piece from white alabaster and polished until the stone shone.

Servants were everywhere, carrying baskets and pots of food to the kitchen where the cooks had been preparing meals made with rare ingredients which the peasants had never tasted before. A train of servants were working their way down the red carpet, removing every speck of dust. Through the ornate hallways of the house, Ti Kuai Li could see black and red lacquer tables arranged with delicate porcelain eating dishes. Nobody noticed the stranger in the midst of all this preparation.

As Ti Kuai Li stepped forward he heard a crunching beneath his feet as the ground moved. He lifted the carpet to reveal a layer of rice as deep as a hand. The carpet stretched down through the garden and out of the arched gateway to the house. Word had spread through the villages and a crowd of beggars waited patiently around the gates of the house, their arms reaching out to the guests who began to filter through. In his torn trousers and jacket and carrying his begging bowl, Ti Kuai Li walked up the wide stairs to the alabaster door. He was immediately held back by two servants and questioned by a guard:

'Who told you to enter this house? Get back beyond the gates where you belong.'

'My family hasn't eaten for days, I have only come to ask for leftover food and whatever you have they will eat,' said Ti Kuai Li as he raised his bowl to the guard.

One of the servants knocked the bowl from his hands while the others laughed to see the beggar so helpless. Then the guard struck Ti Kuai Li across his face and head, vicious blows that sent him reeling down the stone steps, spattering blood on their clean surface. As he eased himself back to his feet, Ti Kuai Li took a handful of rice from the floor, but the guard gripped his wrist so tightly he was forced to drop it.

Meanwhile, guests were arriving at the house and to avoid them witnessing this commotion the servants pulled Ti Kuai Li to one side. In a fierce hushed voice the guard spoke to him,

'We would rather feed our pigs than give you food. We would leave you here to rot, only your sight and smell would offend our honoured guests.'

Ti Kuai Li would not be quietened:

'The rice you have thrown on the floor for the rich to walk on would cost a thousand shi. All I want is enough to fill this bowl. You should beware of mistreating the poor and insulting beggars.'

The authority with which he spoke enraged his attackers who kicked him with such vicious strength he could not move. They turned their backs on him and returned to wait upon the party. While this attack was being made the beggars surrounding the archway had crept into the gardens, concerned for this man who had spoken out for the poor. They begged him not to provoke the rich since the death of a beggar would mean nothing to them.

The sound of feasting and excited voices carried from the house into the gardens. The party had started and the servants continued to file through the hallways with trays of suckling pigs, glazed ducks and chickens, steaming crabs and prawns, aromatic fish and vegetables, and noodles and rice piled high in porcelain bowls. The wealthiest and most influential aristocrats, landowners and merchants sat with K'uang Tzu Lien and as they ate their dishes were continuously filled by ever watchful servants. Suddenly, cries of pain broke through the laughter and echoed throughout the hallways. The porcelain dishes became as hot as a furnace and they fell from the blistered hands of the wealthy. The servants dropped their platters of food and those who reached for a wine to soothe their mouths felt their fingers burn against the porcelain cups.

Slowly the food began to move as maggots emerged from the body of the suckling pig, from the mouth of the fish and from under the mounds of noodles. Before long there were thousands of maggots crawling across the table. K'uang Tzu Lien screamed for the head cook who ran to his side, and then his master hit him across the face.

'You have disgraced me in front of my guests and you'll pay for this trick. Clear this away, fill these tables with food again.'

The servants descended on the tables, clearing away, sweeping down the tables and calming the guests. Fresh bowls of rice and plates of poultry and sweet smelling pastries were hurriedly laid on the tables. Once more cries of disgust rose from the top table. The bowls of rice had turned to a mass of maggots and so many maggots wriggled under the skins of the ducks and chickens they looked ready to burst.

By now all the guests from the other hallways had gathered round the top table. Shocked by what they saw and insulted by this reception, they whispered to each other about K'uang Tzu Lien:

'How can he do this to us, his guests?'

'What an insult, this will never be forgotten.'

'What evil trick has K'uang Tzu Lien played?'

K'uang Tzu Lien was shamed in front of this influential company. At first he was silent and then he was struck by an idea. 'My guard told me of an evil beggar causing trouble outside my house. Some say they cast magic spells – this is his work!'

And so K'uang Tzu Li was led outside to the crumpled form of Ti Kuai Li. His servants pushed aside the beggars who had crowded round to protect him and dragged the immortal to their master's feet.

'Who are you? Where have you come from?' demanded K'uang Tzu Lien.

'I am only a beggar who heard of your banquet and came to beg for food. I am of no importance and only begged for leftovers that would be thrown to the pigs, and yet your guards beat me and left me lying in my own blood.'

Ti Kuai Li's body shook violently, he vomited blood and then lay still before the rich man and the crowd of beggars and servants. Ti Kuai Li was dead and the order was given to bury him. K'uang Tzu Lien returned to reassure his guests at the banquet but the beggars who had witnessed the murder of Ti Kuai Li were not prepared to let him get away with it.

More than thirty beggars walked to the nearby town of Hunan to report the murder to the just police commissioner, Chao Shen Chiao. They waited patiently in the walled yard of his office until Chao Shen Chiao stood in the middle of them and heard their story. He stood attentively, nodding as each beggar added a new comment or piece of information. After hearing their story he made a brief pronouncement.

'He is a wealthy man but this does not buy my protection. Bring me my sedan chair, we are paying him a visit.'

When they arrived at K'uang Tzu Lien's house a crowd of servants had gathered around the body which lay close to the alabaster door. Everyone had tried to lift the immortal's lifeless body, even five of the strongest guards had combined their strength to lift him but no-one could do so. There was a cry from the back of the crowd,

'Make way for the old gentleman of Hunan.'

The crowd pulled aside to make way for the respected magistrate who went straight to Ti Kuai Li's body and knelt at his side. He called into the crowd for a Taoist teacher and an elderly man in a blue robe stepped forward.

'Please examine him, teacher,' asked Chao Shen Chiao, 'and tell me if there is anything unusual.'

The teacher walked slowly around the body and then examined the pockets in Ti Kuai Li's torn jacket. He pulled out a crumpled piece of red paper and read out the words written on it for all to hear.

'Do not make Kuang Tzu Lien pay for this crime with his life. Make him sweep the roads leading from this house to every village and town in this province. He must learn that the rich cannot abuse the poor.'

The magistrate took the paper from the teacher and read the faded signature at the bottom. It was signed Ti Kuai Li. He turned to his police escort,

'Arrest Kuang Tzu Lien, bring him to me.'

Kuang Tzu Lien was forced to kneel at the magistrate's feet. 'An immortal has been killed at your command. I hold you guilty. Are you going to pay with your money or with your life?'

'Take everything I have,' replied K'uang Tzu Lien fearfully, 'I have gold, silver, jewels, my house, my servants. I will give it all for my life.'

'You have made your choice,' answered Chao Shen Chiao. 'Your remaining days will be spent as a road sweeper. You will never again have this power over the poor.'

K'uang Tzu Lien's arms were tied together and he was led away in chains through the jeering crowd. After he had gone the beggars tried to lift Ti Kuai Li's body and were startled to find it was as light as a feather. His body was laid in the shade of a tree while orders were given for a coffin to be brought.

After permission had been given to bury the body on a nearby hillside the whole town turned out to pay respect to the Immortal. But when the coffin was lifted it felt empty. The lid was opened but there was nothing inside. A cry rose from the graveside,

'Someone has stolen our Immortal. He was in our care. We will all be crossed by bad fortune.'

The anxious crowd surged forward to look into the coffin while a messenger ran to tell Chao Shen Chiao what had happened. But the wise magistrate was not perturbed.

'Tell the people of the town they should not worry, they have done nothing wrong. Ti Kuai Li's body may have gone but his spirit is always with us. When you need him, he will be there.'

The magistrate was right. Ti Kuai Li had changed his body into smoke and risen far into the clouds. While the townspeople were mourning his death he had returned to the Immortals' bridge where his friends were waiting to hear his story.

The God of War

Empires wax and wane; states fall apart and re-form. When the Han dynasty fell to corruption, vice and greed, many contenders arose to dispute their right to the Mandate of Heaven. The Middle Kingdom was rent by warfare, brigandry and violence and no one was safe. Men set themselves up as saviours of the common people, but this was only a ruse. Their real interest was warfare and looting. The land mourned, the people lamented.

The great Han dynasty's fall was hastened by the misrule of two Emperors, Huan and Ling. Under the former, eunuchs arose whose sole motivation was personal gain. Under the second of these two Emperors, Ling, the eunuchs took full control, ousting the only two remaining honest advisers and leading the Emperor into a life of debauchery and ignorance.

But Heaven does not rest in such times. Omens and signs were everywhere. One day the Emperor went in state to visit one of the Great Halls. As he came near to the Throne of the Son of Heaven, a swirling whirlwind roared through the hall and from the roof beam descended a terrible black snake, vast and coiled. The dreaded serpent settled upon the very Throne of the Son of Heaven. Seeing this the Emperor collapsed and was rushed from the Hall. When soldiers entered to attack the vile snake, no trace was to be found of it. Instead, hail, thunder and rain beyond belief crashed down upon the capital, terrifying all who beheld it.

Other signs were sent. Earthquakes, tidal waves that swept away entire villages and towns on the coast. Hens became cocks and strange vapours seeped out from under the Throne and were to be seen ascending and descending the Imperial stairways.

Yet the Emperor, alarmed by these portents, failed to correct his ways and fell to relying more and more upon the sycophantic eunuchs who surrounded him. As a result, the Empire began to fall apart, torn asunder by rebellions and violence, lack of justice and the absence of men of true virtue at the helm.

At this time someone was born who was destined to change this world and to be loved by Heaven. His clan name was Chang Sheng, but he is better known by the name he gave himself, Kuan Yu. He was born into an ordinary family, who tried to follow the correct ways of piety and reverence in times when such things had been forgotten.

Chang Sheng was forever getting into trouble. His nature was adventurous and his companions wild. He was of immense strength and seemed not to know fear. This characteristic in a man may be deemed worthy; in a child it is dangerous and his parents feared he would never grow to maturity, such were the risks he took and the troubles he landed in.

Finally, exasperated beyond belief, they locked him in his room to prevent any further adventures. They might as well have tried to prevent the sun rising. Chang Sheng soon found a way out of his room, and enjoying the freedom and the darkness of night he set off to explore the town once again.

Wandering aimlessly around, he found himself in a strange quarter of the town. From a simple house he heard crying and weeping. Peering over the wall, he found an old man and an old woman in great distress. Chang Sheng climbed up and enquired of the old couple what had happened to cause them such unhappiness.

The old man told Chang Sheng that he and his wife had but one child, a daughter, born to them late in their lives. To their great joy, she had become engaged to the grandson of one of their oldest friends and all seemed set for a happy marriage.

But then, one day, the uncle of the local Prefect had ridden past their house. Espying the young woman he had desired her and had ordered his attendants to seize her and carry her off to his mansion. The old man and old woman had gone to the Prefect and appealed for help, but the Prefect had simply refused to see them. With the Prefect taking such an attitude, no one in the town would help them. They had tried to reach their daughter, but it was impossible, for the mansion was heavily guarded. They were now in despair.

When Chang Sheng heard their sad story he felt anger rising within him. He knelt before the old couple and vowed before the Earth god and the gods of the neighbourhood that he would avenge this wrong. So saying he slipped back over the wall and made his way under cover of darkness to the official's mansion. Climbing over the wall, he dropped silently into the courtyard and froze while he listened for the guards. However, all was quiet.

He soon found a door open and slipped inside. Hearing voices in a room off the main corridor, he made his way stealthily towards the doorway. Peering through a crack in the doorway he saw not only the Prefect but also his uncle, joking and laughing together. On the far wall opposite hung an ancient sword – no doubt an heirloom of some great ancestor.

'How fitting,' thought Chang Sheng, 'that with this ancient sword these filthy offspring of a noble house will be purged.'

He swung the door open and before either man had a chance to realize what was upon them, Chang Sheng was across the room in one bound. His foot hit the wall and he turned at the very moment that his hand fell upon the sword. With one swipe he decapitated the Prefect and with one further swing of the sword he despatched the uncle.

Chang Sheng left the house at speed, but not before guards saw him and came running. He leapt the wall and was off down the narrow alleyways before the mansion doors were even opened. But he had been seen and his description was soon out amongst the town guards. Only by smuggling himself out in a cart did he escape the town. Then, realizing that his life was now in gravest danger, he headed for the pass into Shensi, into an area where he knew the law had broken down and warlords ruled. Here, he thought, he would be safe.

Travelling only at night, he made slow progress towards Tung Kuan Pass and Shensi. Approaching the border, he was still some distance off when the officials spotted him and gave chase. He lost them but began to despair that he could ever escape.

But Heaven was pleased with him. The Prefect and his uncle had abused the powers bestowed upon them for many years. They had oppressed the people, stolen what was not theirs, humiliated many fine and old families and corrupted the young with their licentious ways. Heaven's favour had long since been withdrawn. The very next morning, Chang Sheng knelt by a strange stream he found in the mountains, and washed his face, hot from the chase. Looking into the water he saw his face reflected back. Except it was no longer his old face. The water had changed him beyond recognition. His skin was a dark red and all his features had changed totally. The gods had expressed their blessing and favour. It is in this form that he is worshipped to this day.

Later that day he strolled up to the border guards who demanded to know his name.

'My name is Kuan Yu,' he said, and without any further ado, they let him through. And it was thus that he acquired his new name, the name that was to ring down through time.

Kuan Yu meets his sworn brothers

Some years later, Kuan Yu arrived in the town of Chu Chou near Beijing. In the market place of Chu Chou there was a butcher of immense strength and size named Chang Fei. He was eight feet tall, with the eyes of a panther and the beard of a tiger. When he roared it was as if the thunder spoke. All morning he had been chopping and selling his meat. When noon came he lowered the meat in a bucket into the well to keep it cool and then lifted a great rock on top of the well, completely sealing it. Jokingly he shouted out, 'Anyone who can lift that off can have the meat free of charge!'

Kuan Yu heard the challenge and took it for just that. Strolling to the well, he lifted the rock as if it were nothing more than a pebble. He hauled up the bucket and lifted the entire load onto his shoulder. Chang Fei gave a great cry of astonishment and made off after him. Kuan Yu ran with the bucket and the meat bouncing around on his shoulder. Chang Fei ran as if his life depended upon it. Kuan Yu, slowed down by the bucket, was soon overtaken by Chang Fei and a violent fight broke out. No one dared try and separate them for they were both enormous men and the strength of their blows would have felled any ordinary man at once.

Just as it seemed that they would beat each other to death, a wandering sandal seller named Liu Pei chanced upon the scene. Being a man of no fear even though he was of no great stature, he leapt in and separated the two giants – for Kuan Yu was himself nine feet tall, with a great beard, a face the colour of dark red wine, eyes which were scarlet and eyebrows like silkworms. Once he had them apart, he sat them down, gave them a draught of wine each and set to talking with them.

Soon the three men discovered much in common. A hatred of the corrupt officials who were ruining the country. A loathing for the rebels who had usurped the power of the Han dynasty only to bring war, suffering and misery upon the common people. By the end of the evening they had become bosom friends and promised to meet the next day at Chang Fei's peach orchard to formalize their vow to fight together.

The next day saw the three of them in the peach orchard, with a black ox and a white horse, and copious wine for offerings.

Sacrificing the ox and horse, the three friends bowed their heads as the smoke of the burnt offering rose to Heaven and together made the same vow.

'We three, Liu Pei, Kuan Yu and Chang Fei are of different families and clans, yet we swear brotherhood and promise to help each other at all times and under all circumstances to achieve one goal. We shall rescue each other in times of difficulty, we will come to each other's aid in times of peril. We swear to serve only the true State and to defend the common people. We care not that we were born on different days, in different months of diverse years. We ask only that we may die together on the same day, of the same month of the same year. May Heaven who rules over all, and Earth that sustains all hear this vow and if we turn aside from righteousness or forget kindliness, may Heaven smite us dead.'

They rose and saluted Liu Pei as their elder brother. Slaughtering many oxen, they invited three hundred villagers to join them in the feast. There they explained their plans and asked for those who would join them to restore order to the chaos of the country. All three hundred begged to be allowed to join them, and before the week was out the three friends had a force five hundred strong. But no horses. Nor any weapons of value.

As they gathered, keen of intention but devoid of means, two horse traders came into the town with a herd of horses bound for the market at Changshan. Finding willing and eager purchasers right there, the two traders were only too happy to sell. Then came armourers, drawn by news of the growing army. For Chang Fei they made an eighteen foot long spear; for Kuan Yu, a long, curved sword named Black Dragon and for Liu Pei a double-handled sword. In this way, Heaven arms those who seek to restore justice to the land. Armed and with horses for transport, the band moved off to fight for the Han against the rising tide of rebellion. Offering their services to the local Prefect, they were soon despatched to rescue one city after another from the raids of the rebels.

The Battle Against the Chang brothers

But their foes were not just mortal flesh and blood. One of the first against whom they rode was Chang Pao, magician and Taoist sage. The Book of Heaven had been revealed to him and his two brothers by the immortal of the Southern Land of Wonder. They were told that if they studied the book well, they could convert the whole world and bring great peace to all under Heaven.

The Chang brothers studied and soon were able to heal, fight evil spirits and raise up unearthly forces. Their fame spread and they soon established followers whose affairs were guided by chief disciples of the Chang brothers. Such acclaim soon persuaded the Chang brothers that they could rise and overthrow the Emperor. They wielded their followers into tight knit bands and began to speak openly of a new dynasty. They proclaimed that the colour of this new dynasty was to be yellow, and soon their followers were wearing yellow headbands to signify the coming of the new rule.

It was against such forces that the three sworn brothers, Liu Pei, Kuan Yu and Chang Fei, rode. On their first encounter, magic foiled them. Charging against Chang Pao's men, they were close to defeating them when Chang Pao loosened his hair and began his incantations. Immediately the wind rose, whipping into the faces of the three sworn brother soldiers. Then it descended a dark cloud which made it impossible for anyone to see. Disoriented and confused, they could only retreat from the field.

With the aid of a magician of their own in their midst, the three sworn brothers plotted their revenge, knowing that if they attacked Chang Pao on the next day he would resort to similar tactics.

The next day dawned and Liu Pei advanced to attack Chang Pei. Meanwhile two of the sworn brothers, Kuan Yu and Chang Fei, had taken to the hills high above and stationed themselves either side of a ravine, armed with arrows, swords, spears – and barrels full of pig's blood, dog's offal and all manner of dreadful stuff.

When Chang Pao's troops clashed with Liu Pei, the evil magician immediately summoned the aid of demons who stirred up the elements, sending sand flying in vast clouds into the faces of the enemy and hurling pebbles at the valiant troops of Liu Pei. When this did not stop the attack, Chang Pao summoned horsemen and soldiers from the skies, who swept down upon the troops, terrifying them with their grinning skulls and demonic forms. When Liu Pei gave the order to retreat, his men were only too ready to comply. But instead of rushing off into the plains, Liu Pei's men retreated into the long ravine, above which the other two sworn brothers were waiting. Chang Pao's men pushed the attack and the evil forces, ghosts, demons and unnaturally disturbed elements, swept into the ravine after them.

On a given signal, trumpets blared out from either side and Kuan Yu and Chang Fei's men began to rain down pots filled with the blood and offal, which burst as they hit the ground around the enemy, scattering their foul contents widely. As the contents spilled out, the cloud of disturbed elements and ghostly army fell to pieces. The horsemen of the skies fell to the ground as pieces of white paper and the sand and the pebbles ceased their onslaught as the wind died away.

Seeing that his own magic was out-gunned, Chang Pao turned and fled, leaving his men to their fate.

But it proved to be the turning point in the fight against the Chang brothers. One by one they were captured or died at the hand of their own followers and within a short period, that rebellion at least was quenched.

But there were many disturbances within the land. For year after year the three sworn brothers fought against immense odds. They also had to fight against the jealousy of those who were supposed to be on their side and against the machinations of the palace eunuchs who sought to split up the famous three.

In turn they were offered positions of great power; lordships, command over vast armies; even minor kingdoms. At times they were tempted, but always, whenever it came between them and their other sworn brothers, they gave up all to be free to fight for what was right.

Nor were they always successful. Many battles were lost as well as many won. The tides of fortune rolled this way and that, but gradually Liu Pei arose as one of the greatest commanders and began to gain control over swathes of the country. He ended as ruler of a small kingdom. In his struggles he could always rely upon the loyalty of his two sworn blood brothers and nothing would prevent them coming to his aid.

Tsao Tsao's trick

At one time Tsao Tsao, a great opponent of Liu Pei, rose to be ruler of a state and tried to trap Kuan Yu into abandoning his fidelity to Liu Pei. Tsao Tsao had defeated Liu Pei in battle and shattered his forces. Kuan Yu had taken Liu Pei's two wives to safety in the city of Hsiapi. He waited for word of the fate of his friend, but none came and he feared that Liu Pei was dead. Meanwhile, Tsao Tsao wished to capture the city and to humiliate Kuan Yu, thus breaking up the famous trio.

To do this he hatched a plot with Chang Liao, a former friend of Kuan Yu. They decided to send back some soldiers of Kuan Yu's who had deserted. They were to pretend that they had changed their minds and wished to rejoin Kuan Yu's army. Once they were safely inside the city, the next stage of the plan, a feigned attack, would take place to lure Kuan Yu from the city.

All went according to plan. The deserters returned and after initial doubts were welcomed back into Kuan Yu's army. Shortly after, five companies of troops came before the city walls and, hurling insults at Kuan Yu, sought to draw him out into battle. At first he just ignored them, but soon their vicious comments and treacherous slurs drove him to great anger. Calling out his three best companies of soldiers, he ordered the city gate to open and rode out to do battle. At first the attackers put up a stiff resistance, but then at a prearranged signal, they feigned fear and fled, drawing the enraged Kuan Yu after them. Some distance from the city, the attackers turned and stood their ground, battling hard with Kuan Yu's men. Again, at a pre-arranged signal the attackers retreated, drawing Kuan Yu further away. Soon he found himself over twenty miles from the city. Suddenly he became aware of how foolish he had been. Turning, he sought to fight his way back to the city, but found he was cut off by further companies of the enemy. Meanwhile, inside the city, the treacherous troops who had returned opened the city gates and allowed the enemy, Tsao Tsao, to enter. Soon the city was given over to looting, pillage and fire.

When Kuan Yu saw the smoke rising from the direction of the city, he knew he had lost.

Then his former friend, Chang Liao, came to see him under a flag of negotiation.

Chang Liao lost no time in pointing out that Kuan Yu had no hope of winning against the troops ranged against him and with his city fallen.

Kuan Yu replied, 'Though escape is impossible, I am not worried. I look upon death as simply going home. You should now depart and leave me to prepare for this fight.'

But Chang Liao debated with him late into the night. He pointed out that Kuan Yu had taken a vow to guard Liu Pei's wives and family. If he now allowed himself to die, no matter how gloriously, he would fail to honour that pledge.

By daybreak, Kuan Yu had agreed to surrender and was led before the victorious Tsao Tsao who through deceit had accomplished what would have been impossible by honourable means. But Tsao Tsao had not finished with Kuan Yu's honour yet.

Shortly after, the victorious army left to march home. In the train came Kuan Yu, still guarding his blood brother's family, and especially the two lovely wives of Liu Pei. That night, when the army stopped, Tsao Tsao deliberately housed Kuan Yu and the two wives in one room, hoping thereby to be able to discredit Kuan Yu and spread rumours of his faithlessness.

But Kuan Yu was a match for his cunning. All night he stood before the doorway of the room, holding a lighted candle so that all might see him and with his sword drawn to protect the honour of the women within. Not once did his eyelids close. Not once did fatigue overcome him. Tsao Tsao seeing this realized that he had seriously misjudged Kuan Yu and his respect and admiration for him grew. When the army arrived at the capital, Kuan Yu maintained his respectful watch over the women and his renown spread far and wide.

Tsao Tsao recognized Kuan Yu for the great man that he was. Despite their differences, a friendship grew between them, for Kuan Yu found Tsao Tsao to be a man of integrity. He even returned Kuan Yu's beloved horse to him. Kuan Yu began to fight for Tsao Tsao and was instrumental in winning battles and cities for his new lord.

But when Kuan Yu found that Liu Pei was alive and fighting on the other side from Tsao Tsao, Kuan Yu returned to his former loyalty. Kuan Yu tried to tell Tsao Tsao that he must return to his friend. But Tsao Tsao prevented Kuan Yu from seeing him. So it was that one night Kuan Yu bundled the women into a carriage and taking only a small handful of loyal soldiers, broke out of the capital city. No sooner did Tsao Tsao learn of his escape than a commander offered to go and capture him. But Tsao Tsao recognized that loyalty was the very heart of Kuan Yu and forbade any pursuit.

Tsao Tsao and the ambush

Years later, Kuan Yu was to return this favour. Tsao Tsao's army had been all but wiped out in a great struggle and with just a few men he had managed to escape. Pursued by the victorious army of yet another contender for the Throne, Tsao Tsao had taken refuge in a forest which was then set alight by his foe.

Charging out of the forest, Tsao Tsao found himself having to ride into a narrow defile. 'Surely any sensible man would use this place to attack me,' he said, laughing. No sooner were the words out of his mouth than a bomb exploded beside him and there stood Kuan Yu and a select group of fellow warriors.

'Now it is only left for us to fight to the death. Prepare your-selve,' said Tsao Tsao to his followers.

But Chang Liao replied, 'It is well known that Kuan Yu is harsh on the proud but generous to the humble. He hates the powerful but loves the weak. He discriminates between affection and hatred, and in all his actions is concerned with justice and right-eousness. You, Sire, have been kind to him. He will recall this I am sure.'

When Kuan Yu and Tsao Tsao came face to face, Kuan Yu did indeed recall the generosity and honour of Tsao Tsao. With tears in his eyes he gave the order to his men to break formation. For a short while Kuan Yu rode around, reorganizing his men into battle form. As he did so, Tsao Tsao and his men slipped past. By the time Kuan Yu had re-ordered his men, there was no sign of Tsao Tsao. Thus did Kuan Yu repay the kindness he had been shown.

The death of Kuan Yu

The years rolled on and Kuan Yu had a son who joined him in his battles. A new usurper arose, one Sun Chuan, who rode out against Kuan Yu, faithful defender of the Han. In battle after battle, the advantage swung from side to side, but gradually Kuan Yu's forces were worn down until he found himself alone with but three hundred men in the city of Maicheng. Sun Chuan knew he had him trapped and he posted guards on all the routes, great and small, that led away from the city.

Inside the city, Kuan Yu decided to try and break out with a handful of men, to seek help from other armies who might come to the rescue of Maicheng. Side by side with his son, Kuan Yu rode out, mounted for the last time upon his famous steed, Red Hare. Few were the men left to accompany him, yet not one questioned the wisdom of their going. Under cover of darkness they made good progress at first, but not for long. Some ten miles from the city they were ambushed. Kuan Yu and his son Kuan Ping charged, their great swords raised and terror struck the hearts of the ambushers. But escape from this first attack was only the beginning of that long night. A second and then a third ambush took them by surprise. Valiantly they struggled on, fighting to left and to right; now before them, now behind. With only a score of men left, Kuan Yu and Kuan Ping broke through the last ambush only to find themselves attacked by yet another ambush. Here the ground was soft and the attackers armed with hooks and nets with which they entrapped the horses and brought them down. Kuan Yu fell from his steed and before Kuan Ping could come to his rescue, they were both seized and taken prisoner.

When they were dragged before Sun Chuan, the usurper tried to win them over to his side. But his attempts at treachery were cut short by Kuan Yu.

'You naive youth!' Kuan Yu said. 'You red-bearded rat! In the Peach Orchard I vowed with my brothers to defend the Han dynasty. Do you think I would join my forces with a traitor such as you? I am trapped by your evil doing, but I can only die once. So end your tittle-tattle.'

Sun Chuan saw that words would have no effect. He feared Kuan Yu and therefore gave the order for the execution of father and son.

Father and son together knelt side by side. Neither uttered a word. Neither broke the vows they had made. Together they were executed. It was the year 219 AD. Kuan Yu was fifty eight years old. His faithful steed Red Hare refused to leave the place and would take no nourishment. Rather, he stood beside the fallen body of his friend and master until, overcome by starvation, he too died.

But memory of Kuan Yu did not die. As one poet has said:

Without equal was our Lord Kuan,
Above all others he rose up, the best amongst the best.
Godlike and terrible in war, he was kindly and gentle in peace.
Glorious as the sun at noon,
Radiant as the noblest of all times,
He remains, the illumination of all others, for all ages,
A sign of virtue to every generation.

The Legend of Kuan Yu and his sworn brothers

Over the succeeding centuries, Kuan Yu has become more loved and more honoured. In the year 1102, the Emperor Hui Tsung elevated him with the title King of Military Pacification, in recognition of the struggle through warfare for justice and peace that was the hallmark of Kuan Yu's life.

It was with the elevation to Grand Emperor of Heaven by Emperor Wan Li in 1594 that he gained his official title of Kuan Ti (Ti means Heavenly Emperor). In 1813 there was an attempt upon the life of the Emperor Chia Ching. The assassins tried to murder the Emperor within the walls of his own palace, attacking the imperial quarters. When the attack failed, the guards swore that they had seen Kuan Ti himself, sword raised, standing at the entrance to the imperial quarters, defending the Emperor's life. Likewise, in 1856, Kuan Ti is supposed to have appeared in the Heavens, leading a Heavenly army, during a great battle against the Taiping rebels who were seeking to overthrow the Ching dynasty. Such was the gratitude that the Emperor and the whole Manchu Court felt towards Kuan Ti that they erected temples to his honour in every town and the local officials were expected to go and pay their respects to him once every year.

But long before the Court had recognized his powers, Kuan Ti was already revered and worshipped by the ordinary people as a defender of the weak, the poor and the helpless against oppressors. Pictures and statues of him are to be found all over China. Sometimes he stands beside Red Hare, his faithful horse, sword in hand. Beside him are his son Kuan Ping, who carries the Imperial Seal of the Grand Emperor, and his faithful attendant Chou Chang who carries a halberd.

Kuan Ti is not just revered as a god of war and of justice in this world. He is also one of the most powerful exorcists, and no ghost or evil spirit can abide his presence, whether in image or even acted upon a stage. There are numerous stories of his powers, of which the following is but one.

The story of the Romance of the Three Kingdoms, the account of the struggles in which Liu Pei, Cheng Fei and Kuan Yu were caught up, is one of the most popular subjects of Chinese theatre and opera. Thus every touring group of performers knows scenes from Kuan Yu's life.

One day a group of famous performers in Peking were at rehearsal when a young man rode up with an invitation. The invitation, sent by a young woman of excellent birth, requested that the actors follow the servant and attend a great party which was to be held at a mansion near to Peking. Always on the lookout for a few extra coins, the actors agreed and following the servant they travelled out of the city into the nearby countryside.

It was night time by the time they reached the mansion. Set back from the road, it was ablaze with lights and filled with people, all of whom seemed young, happy and full of delight at being together. Upon entering, another servant took the actors to one side and said that his mistress had said that they were only to perform love songs and scenes of romantic love. Under no circumstances were they to perform any scene in which a god or goddess might appear and, most especially, no scene with Kuan Ti in it.

Agreeing to this, and looking forward to an enjoyable evening, for the wine was flowing freely and food was everywhere, the actors began to perform. The audience certainly seemed to appreciate their performances and called constantly for more, more. At first the actors thought that they would soon be fed or offered drink. But as the evening went on, they found themselves forced to perform but for no reward. Whenever they stopped, they were urged to continue. Whenever they asked for food or drink, they were told 'later, later.'

As the night turned towards morning, the actors were exhausted and very, very annoyed. Finally they decided that just to spite their hostess, they would disobey her request and perform a scene from the life of Kuan Ti. No sooner had the actor wearing the distinctive red face and full beard of Kuan Ti appeared on stage than the whole scene changed before their very eyes. Gone were the revellers; gone was the food and drink; gone were the bright lights; gone was the very house itself. To their astonishment and considerable consternation, the actors found themselves standing on top of a new grave. Leaping down, they read the inscription and discovered that they had been lured to perform by the ghost of a young woman who had died very recently. It was obvious that they had been entertaining the ghosts of those who die young and without Kuan Ti's intervention, they might never have escaped from their clutches.

The Old Man's Warning

Weng Jen was a talented but bad-tempered feng shui master who travelled widely giving advice on the siting of graves, houses and villages. It was not unusual for a family to move house or to demolish part of a building on his word.

One hot summer he was asked to assess a burial site in a mountainous area far from his home. It had taken three weeks to walk to the graveyard outside a village and a day to carry out a full reading. He had spent the night in a village inn and the next day began his journey home with his compass, ruler and papers tied in a red bag. On the second day of his return journey the sun had been beating down but he had not passed a stream nor a well after eight hours of walking. He was now in the foothills of the mountains and could see a woman and her children winnowing grain on the plain ahead of him.

The family stopped their work as they watched the stranger approach and call out to them:

'Do you have any water? I am exhausted and cannot carry on unless I have something to drink.'

The woman walked to the shade of a nearby tree and uncorked a pitcher of cool water. She held the pitcher under her arm, poured out a bowl of water and walked up to Weng Jen. Just before she handed it to him she picked up chaff from the floor and scattered it across the water.

Weng Jen grabbed the bowl from her without thanks. Not only had she insulted him by throwing chaff in the water but now he had to blow the chaff aside each time he need to take a mouthful. As he emptied the bowl he planned his revenge.

'Do you live far from here?' he asked.

The woman pointed to a small, ramshackle house in the distance.

'That's where I live with my three sons but I cannot afford to repair it. My husband died three years ago and now I spend my days just finding enough food for us to eat.'

The feng shui master studied the distant house and the land around it before he spoke:

'I am not surprised you have such bad fortune, the feng shui of your house and of the surrounding land will badly affect your prosperity and your health. This is a site which will continue to bring you misfortune, but I know how all this can change. Beyond that distant mountain is an uninhabited house surrounded by overgrown fields but do not be deterred by its condition for the site has excellent feng shui.'

The family bowed in gratitude before the feng shui master and without further conversation he lifted his red bag and left them. As punishment, he had directed them to a notorious site known as 'Five Ghosts Dead Place', a site so full of misfortune that the young boys would be unlikely to reach the age of twenty.

Five years later Weng Jen returned to the mountain to see if the family had survived. The mother had seen him and ran out to greet him.

'Do you remember me?' asked Weng Jen.

'How could we forget you?' replied the woman. 'It was your wise advice that led us to this place and to our good fortune. Our lands are fruitful and my sons successful. I have two boys who have been accepted for government service and one who is going to train with a wise teacher. None of this would have been possible without you. Please join us to eat and to rest.'

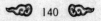 140

While Weng Jen ate the rice and vegetables grown by the woman he quietly surveyed the house. The walls were newly plastered, the roof well laid, and the furniture simple but comfortable. Nothing had changed in the landscape around the house and there was still bad feng shui. He wondered how she could have flourished on this doomed site.

'I cannot understand why your life has been so lucky,' he told her. 'I sent you to an inauspicious site and yet good fortune has rained on you. What have you done for Heaven to bless you like this?'

The woman was startled by this admission, 'What did I do to anger you? Why did you want to punish me?'

'When I passed through here five years ago, I was desperate for water. Instead of offering clean water you threw chaff upon the surface to insult me.'

'What a mistake you have made,' replied the woman. 'When I saw you, you were weak from the heat and desperately thirsty. The water was very cold but you would have drunk it quickly and the shock would have been great. To protect you, I placed chaff on the water so you would have to clear the surface each time you took a sip.'

The feng shui master smiled as he heard the story.

'Now I understand why you and your sons have been blessed by good fortune. I sent you to a desolate place but Heaven has recognized your compassion and blessed you.'

5
Buddhist

The Phonenix and the Bat

Once upon a time, the Lord Buddha was meditating, protected by the Phoenix, who never sleeps but who guards the Buddha night and day. A strange spirit of discord known as the Old White Bat flew in, squeaking and flapping its wings. This interrupted the meditations of the Buddha and therefore the Phoenix leapt upon the Old White Bat and tore it to pieces.

The Buddha was distressed by this zeal of the Phoenix and, to punish him, sent him to be reborn upon earth in the form of a white eagle. This was a most difficult incarnation within which to work for salvation from his previous action, for the eagle is itself a violent creature, which lives by the kill. Yet the Phoenix knew he must abide by the precept of taking no life. So the Phoenix sought to control his instincts in the hope of rebirth in a more favourable form. However this was all to no avail. One day he spotted a tortoise on a river bank. Overcome with the desire to kill he swept down, seized the poor tortoise and devoured it there and then.

In the cycle of rebirth, the Buddha decided to provide another opportunity for his faithful servant the Phoenix to redeem himself.

So the Phoenix/White Eagle was reborn as Yue Fei. Yue Fei was the brave and patriotic general under the Southern Sung who in 1140 defeated the invading Mongols. However, he was betrayed by the treachery of the Emperor's adviser – Chin Kuei – who was none other than the poor tortoise the Phoenix had killed in his previous life, and the even more treacherous wife of Chin Kuei was the reborn spirit of the Old White Bat.

The tortoise and the Old White Bat were out for revenge. They told the Emperor that Yue Fei was trying to establish himself as a new Emperor, or that he was in communication with the enemy in order to betray the empire. In fact it was Chin Kuei and his wife who were trying to betray the empire to the enemy and they feared that Yue Fei would find out.

The phoenix in the form of Yue Fei proved himself to have learnt his lesson. Despite the most terrible provocations and the most dreadful betrayals by all around, he remained true to his oath of obedience. He could have raised his army as a rebel and overthrown the Emperor – but he did not. He could have attacked the evil minister Chin Kuei and his wife – but he did not. He could have fled to safety – but he did not. He remained and took the punishment given him, always protesting his total loyalty and showing that on his own back his mother had tattooed 'Loyal even unto death for my country'.

After his execution as a condemned criminal, he had to undergo the most terrible punishments in the eighteen dreadful Buddhist Hells before at long last his countrymen recognized his real virtue and erected a temple over his tomb. When this happened, the Lord Buddha was able to send to the Judges of Hell and demand the soul of Yue Fei, the Phoenix, to be released and to be given back its Phoenix form. The Phoenix who never sleeps continues to guard the Lord Buddha day and night.

But Chin Kuei and his wife had fallen prey to vengeance and violence. For them the cycle of dreadful rebirths has only just begun and they will turn in suffering for eighty thousand rebirths each one as dreadful as the other until they have cleansed themselves of the crime against Yue Fei, the never sleeping Phoenix.

Miao Shan, the goddess of compassion

Long ago, in the kingdom of Hsing Lin, the king of the time, a weak but kindly man, was overthrown by a harsh and brutal usurper. This violent usurper, who dared to go against the Mandate of Heaven, was called Miao Chuang. His Queen was called Pao Te and between them they ruled the land. Although they longed for a son to succeed them and to ensure that their family would rule for centuries to come, the gods would not grant them one because of the bloodshed which had accompanied Miao Chuang's seizure of the throne. Despite the pleading and desperate prayers of the king and queen, of their ministers and numerous priests and sages, the gods refused to grant the royal couple their desire for a son and heir. Indeed, instead of a son, the royal pair were given three daughters. These daughters were most special in their own way, for they were the reincarnated souls of three worthy boys born to a devout Buddhist family who were murdered by brigands. Their young lives having been cut off before they could perform meritorious acts of their own, the three young souls were given a new chance to earn merit. They were born into the most pampered and favourable of circumstances to test how devout they were to Buddhist principles.

So it was that Her Royal Majesty gave birth to three beautiful daughters. The first to be born was called Miao Yen and the second one was called Miao Yin. But it is the last one who is at the heart of our story.

At the very moment of the conception of this last daughter, Queen Pao Te dreamed she had swallowed the moon. The pregnancy was filled with signs of a wondrous event and many commented upon how all the ten thousand species seemed to be in a state of excitement awaiting this royal birth. As the child was about to be borne, the earth itself shook, and the air suddenly seemed to be filled with a wonderful fragrance. It was as if spring had come in an instant, for divine flowers, of outstanding beauty and fragrance, suddenly sprang up all across the land. In addition to these portents, as soon as she came forth from the womb this third daughter, named Miao Shan, was as fresh and clean as if she had been newly washed. Her countenance was of divine beauty and her body was surrounded by Heavenly clouds of many different colours. To all of those present at her birth there was no doubt that she was a goddess. All that is except for her parents. They were still hoping for a son, and thus were furious at the birth of yet another useless daughter. Their anger led them to ignore these signs of divinity, and in their arrogant foolishness, they took against her.

As the years rolled on the king in his disappointment at the lack of a son and heir could only take comfort in the hopes of good marriages for his daughters. His chief minister pointed out that he was bound to gain through marrying off his three beautiful, intelligent, and highly eligible daughters, as he would have a choice of three young men to take over his kingdom. Therefore the king and queen set their hopes on finding eligible marriage partners for their daughters.

Now from an early age, Miao Shan, the youngest daughter, showed that she was no ordinary child. She spurned the frivolities of the Court; the endless chatter about dresses and gossip about the courtiers. She even disdained ordinary childhood pursuits in favour of a life of devotion to Buddha. She spent her time in prayer and meditation. She chose to dress in plain and simple cloth, scorning the rich brocades of the court. Her diet was likewise simple, preferring a bowl of rice and vegetables to the sumptuous feasts of the royal household. In her behaviour and demeanour she showed to those who could see, that she was a Bodhisattva, and many came to love the gentle child from whom the mercy of the Buddha radiated like sunlight. But to her parents and to her sisters, she seemed just odd and difficult; a child whom they could not comprehend; a child who seemed to reject everything which they thought to be important. Rather than open their hearts to her message, they closed their hearts and both feared and resented her.

As she grew to adulthood, her love of charity and kindness earned her the name of Maiden with the Heart of the Buddha. Through her example, her ladies in waiting were brought to faith in the Buddha and turned from their frivolous ways towards a more humble and generous spirit.

Let me give you just one example of the compassion of this wonderful child. She was sitting by herself, meditating in the garden of the palace one evening. Above her sat a cicada who was happily chattering away. The sound of the cicada gradually lulled her off to sleep. In the midst of her dreams she heard a terrible scream. Waking with a start from her slumbers she leaped to her feet to see what creature it could be that was in such distress. She saw that the little cicada had been grabbed by a large praying mantis who had wrapped its legs tightly around the helpless insect.

Desperate to save the creature from the grip of the praying mantis, Miao Shan climbed up onto the wall where, precariously perched, she reached out and freed the cicada from the mantis' hold. Angry at being deprived of its prey, the mantis turned on Miao Shan and viciously attacked her hand. Startled by this, Miao Shan lost her footing on the wall and with a cry fell to the ground, cutting her forehead. Her sisters, hearing her cry out, rushed to her. They found her with blood flowing from the wound on her forehead and sought to comfort her. But Miao Shan merely shrugged her shoulders and said, 'A scar on my forehead is a small price to pay for the life of a cicada.' This is just one example of the generosity of heart which Miao Shan showed every day to all living beings.

But none of this pleased the king and queen. They were not impressed by this gentle soul in their midst and her father determined to find her a husband as soon as he could. He was sure she would soon snap out of her pious behaviour and fulfil his dreams and aspirations for her.

The king had already found desirable husbands for his two eldest daughters and they had been married with great ceremony and much feasting and rejoicing. Now he was determined to find a suitable young man for Miao Shan. However, Miao Shan had her own ideas and they certainly did not include marriage.

Standing before her imperial father, she spoke from the heart:

'Riches and fame are not eternal; glory and magnificence are mere bubbles, illusions. I wish to become a nun and to renounce the world. Even if you force me to work as a servant, I shall never change my mind or my resolve.'

So saying she left her father's presence. Her mother tried to plead with her and brought her again before her father, begging her to reconsider. To this Miao Shan replied:

'I will do as you command if as a result three woes of the world are removed.'

The king was astonished at this and asked her, 'What do you mean by three woes of the world?'

She replied: 'The first woe is that when people are young their faces are fair as a jade moon, but with old age their hair turns white, their faces wrinkle and whether they are active or passive, they are in every way worse off than when they were young.

'The second woe is that a person's body may be lithe and trim, fit and healthy. They may walk with ease, moving like a bird on the wing. But should illness strike they collapse into bed taking no pleasure in anything.

'The third woe is that someone might have a host of friends and relatives, always surrounded by companions and those who are dearest. Then comes the day of death and suddenly this is all at an end. No friend nor relative can take their place.

'So, if being married can help heal these woes, then I will willingly give myself in wedlock. If not, then I ask permission to retire to a life of religious devotion.'

Her father was aghast at this and exploded with rage. He ranted and stormed at her but to no avail. Miao Shan simply stood there, calmly enduring his fearsome wrath. Her mother, seeing her resolve, took her on one side and tried to argue with her.

'What you ask is impossible. Try and be reasonable. We have chosen a good man as your prospective husband. He is a good military man.'

Miao Shan, seeing the genuine concern of her mother, spoke again. 'Mother, if I must marry then I could only marry a doctor.'

Before she could go any further her mother exploded with indignation. 'A doctor! A doctor! That may be a good match for the common people, but what sort of prince would such a person make? How could such a person rule? Why a doctor more that a fine military man?'

Miao Shan spoke again quietly. 'My desire is to heal the world of all its ills; of the chills of winter and the heats of summer; of the fires of lust and the damp of old age; of all sickness. I wish to make all equal regardless of riches and poverty. I want all things to be shared so no one goes without or has more than they need. If I can marry a man who will help me in this, then I shall marry tomorrow.'

Her father again cast her from him, so angry he didn't know what to say. Her mother tried one more time.

'My daughter,' she said, 'is it not a crime for a daughter to disobey her father?'

Miao Shan replied that it was. 'Then, my dear,' argued her mother, 'surely you can see you must obey your father.' Miao Shan remained silent so, thinking she had won on this point, her mother brought her again before her father the king.

The king said, 'You agree that it is a crime to go against the wishes of your father?'

Miao Shan said, 'It is a crime for me to refuse to do what my father earnestly requests of me, but you will simply have to pardon me for I cannot go against higher commands.'

'What higher commands?' bellowed her father.

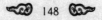

'The commands of Buddha. I wish to become a nun, to attain perfection and gain Buddhahood. Once I have done this, then I will obey you and bring you blessings.'

Her father was beside himself. 'Wretched and useless daughter. Who has ever heard of the daughter of a king becoming a nun? Only the poorest and most ignorant give up all for such a life. Forget this. You will eventually come to your senses and marry whom I chose.'

So saying he decreed that Miao Shan was to be set to work on the most demeaning jobs in the palace and that she was to be given only just enough food and drink to keep her alive. Her sisters seeing her so reduced pleaded with her to change her mind and marry, but they could not prevail against her resolve to take the religious path. When her mother went to intercede with her again, Miao Shan rebuked her, saying:

'Empty things come to an end. I desire what is infinite.'

Her mother realized nothing could shake her resolve so, against her better judgement, asked the king to allow Miao Shan to retire to a nunnery and take up the religious life. The king was furious and he decided that if she was going to go ahead with this life, then she should be made to suffer. Perhaps then she would come to her senses.

He summoned the abbess of the nunnery that Miao Shan had chosen. This was the Nunnery of the White Sparrow, in the prefecture of Ju Chou. He told the abbess that while he was prepared to allow Miao Shan to enter the nunnery, he expected the nuns to make life as difficult and unpleasant as possible for the princess, so that she would come to her senses and return to her home. The abbess, frightened by the power of the king, agreed to do whatever she could to comply with his commands.

Upon the abbess's return, she called all the nuns together and explained that the king's daughter was to join them but that they were to do all in their power to dissuade her from taking up her vocation. The abbess made it quite clear that if they failed, they could expect the wrath of the king to descend upon them. While

 149

some were frightened by this, others were moved by the devotion of this princess to the Buddha life.

When she entered the nunnery, the abbess put Miao Shan to work in the kitchen and ordered that she should be given the most unpleasant tasks, with instructions that if she did not do well there, she would be dismissed at once. Such a lowly and demeaning posting was, of course, exactly what Miao Shan wanted. She set to with a will, but even for her the tasks were demanding ones. In Heaven, the Master of Heaven saw her labours and the difficulties some of the nuns put in her way from spite. Sympathetic to her plight, he called up the god of the North Star and told him to bring the Gods of the Five Sacred Mountains, the Eight Ministers of the Heavenly Dragon and the local Earth gods to her assistance. The Sea Dragon was ordered to dig a well for her, tigers brought firewood while the birds collected vegetables for her, and the gods summoned to her service were to toil in the kitchen at her command.

The result of all this divine help did not go unnoticed in the nunnery. Jealousy was created amongst the more simple and foolish nuns who resented Miao Shan's beauty, her goodness and her rank in the outside world. One nun spoke out against her, saying that she was a trouble maker and would bring disaster upon them all. She told Miao Shan to leave them alone and go back to being a princess, but Miao Shan rebuked her.

'Have you not heard that those who try to obstruct a monastic vocation will suffer torments for innumerable aeons? Do you willingly oppose the Buddhist faith and accept the risks of retribution in the Hells?'

The nun, aghast at this, protested her innocence saying, 'I am under the king's orders. It is not of my choice.'

But despite all this, Miao Shan would not give in. Word soon reached the king, who flew into a temper. He stormed up and down the palace shouting of his ungrateful and wilful daughter, until at last, consumed utterly by his rage, he ordered his Commander of the Palace troops to go immediately to the nunnery and burn it to the ground, killing all the nuns therein. The commander took a force of over five thousand hand picked, ruthless soldiers. Swiftly they moved. Swiftly they surrounded the nunnery. Swiftly they set fire to the surroundings and watched as the flames raced towards the nunnery.

In the nunnery pandemonium broke out, with nuns rushing in all directions. Some found Miao Shan and began abusing her, saying 'This is all your fault.'

Miao Shan knelt before them and said humbly, 'It is true. Destruction would not have come to this nunnery if I had not been here.' Then, horrified at what was happening, she prayed to Buddha. 'Great Sovereign of the Universe. I am the daughter of a king. You were the son of a king. Just as you left your palace to seek enlightenment, taking to the remote hills, so have I left my palace and come to this mountain. Please hear my prayer and rescue your younger sister and her fellow nuns.'

So saying, she pricked the top of her mouth with a bamboo hairpin and spat the blood that flowed into the air. Immediately it transformed into vast rain clouds which poured down upon the raging fires and quenched them to the amazement of all who watched. The nuns were safe. The Commander of the Palace Guards retreated and reported to the king. The king could stand it no more and ordered that Miao Shan be seized, bound in chains and brought back to the palace to be immediately executed. Without a moment to rest, the Commander returned to the nunnery with his troops, seized Miao Shan, bound her hand and foot and bore her off to the palace. On the way, in one last attempt to convince her to rejoin the rich life of the palace, all manner of things were set up along the roadside to remind her of her former circumstance. Music, songs, and great feasts were prepared, but Miao Shan showed nothing but disdain for these worldly things, and passed by with her eyes cast down.

Her mother tried once again to plead with her, but to no avail. The king gave the command that at dawn the next day she was to be executed. But he was overheard by the Earth gods who reported all this to the Master of Heaven. The Master of Heaven summoned the Earth god of the execution square and told him that he was to use all his magic to prevent any wound being inflicted upon the princess. At the moment of her death he was to transform into a tiger and leap out to snatch up her body. He was to bear it away to a safe place, place a pill of immortality in her mouth to prevent her body decaying and then await the return of her soul from its journeys.

The next morning, as dawn broke, the princess was led out into the execution square. The king's warrant arrived for the execution, and the sky began to turn pitch black. As the executioner lifted his sword, a brilliant light fell all around Miao Shan, and the sword fell in pieces upon the ground. When he tried to kill her using a spear, the spear dissolved in his hand. Eventually he had to resort to using a silken cord to strangle her. As her breath died within her, the onlookers scattered in terror as a huge tiger bounded into the square. Roaring and leaping he covered the square in two bounds, seized the body of Miao Shan in his mouth and was gone before any could move or think. The tiger, the Earth god, bore Miao Shan's body to a forest where he laid her down and placed the pill of immortality in her mouth.

Meanwhile her soul had begun its journeys. She awoke from her death sleep to find herself in a terrible, desolate place. 'What is this place?' she asked aloud. 'I was being strangled but a moment ago, and now I find myself in this wasteland, with nothing around me. Not mountains, nor trees, nor rivers. I see no sun or moon in the sky, not even the bright stars. There is no sound – no chirping of birds, or even the sharp yaps of a dog. How can I live here?'

She was answered by a tall young man standing beside her. 'You are in the first of the Eighteen Buddhist Hells. As a reward for your virtue, you are to receive an audience with the Gods of the Hells.'

When Miao Shan arrived before them, she asked 'Who am I that you pay me such attention?'

They said 'We have heard that when you pray all evil disappears. We would like to hear you pray.'

The sights that surrounded her of the souls of the damned, tortured and tormented beyond belief, moved her to profound compassion. She immediately began to pray for those who were in such agony around her. Instantly the Hells began to be transformed. The terrible heat gave way to a pleasant climate. The instruments of torture turned into flowers and trees. Hell became a Paradise and the damned rejoiced at her mercy.

The Kings and judges of Hell went to complain to the Emperor of Hell. 'For there to be justice in the world, there must be both Heaven and Hells. Through the mercy of Miao Shan, the Hells are now the same as Heaven. Thus there can be no true justice. We beseech you, release Miao Shan so that the Hells can once again become the places of punishment and justice can once again be administered.'

The Emperor of Hell agreed and had Miao Shan escorted back to her body. They gave her a peach of immortality to eat which brought her back to life. Upon waking, once more alive, Miao Shan found herself on Hsiang Shan and there she dwelt for many years perfecting herself, realizing her full Bodhisattva nature.

One day she was walking upon the mountain when the Ju Lai Buddha appeared before her. He asked her how she came to be alone in such a place. She replied by telling him all that had befallen her. To her great consternation the Ju Lai Buddha proposed that as he too was alone in the world, they should marry, build themselves a little house and live away the rest of their lives in happiness!

Miao Shan made it quite clear what she thought of that suggestion, and then the Ju Lai Buddha revealed that he had been sent to test her vocation and her determination. The Buddha then invited her to come to a special place set aside for her, where she could perfect herself. This is the island of Pu To Shan in the seas off the coast of China. She consented and was borne there by ministering gods and goddesses.

Miao Shan spent nine years on Pu To Shan, perfecting herself. At the end of nine years, all the gods came to greet her and to salute her wisdom. She asked only that they find her two companions, a virtuous maiden and a worthy young man.

The gods chose for her a young man who from an early age had devoted himself to religious studies as a hermit monk. When this young man, Shan Tsai, was brought before her, she decided to test his devotion to her. She set him to meditate upon a mountain top near to her. Then she commanded the local Earth gods to take up the disguise of being brigands and to storm her part of the mountain top. Instantly, a savage horde appeared at the base of the mountain and came swarming up, apparently intent upon slaying Miao Shan. Miao Shan, feigning distress, rushed up the mountain and as she reached the peak, stumbled and fell down the mountain face. Shan Tsai, seeing this happen, and giving no thought to himself or his own safety, leaped from his peak, plunging down the deep chasm until he reached Miao Shan. When he reached her, he rebuked her for such folly and she rebuked him for being so impetuous. Then she asked him to look down to the very bottom of the chasm and tell her what he saw. Looking down he saw a corpse.

'That is your former body,' said Miao Shan. 'Through your devotion to me, you have been released from your old body and given this immortal body. Now you will be able to walk the clouds, climbing up to Heaven and plunging down to the depths. But from now on you will stay by my side always.'

Kneeling and kowtowing, Shan Tsai thanked her from the bottom of his heart and from that day until this he has never left her side.

Some time later, Miao Shan was scanning the world as her spiritual vision allowed her to do. Looking deep into the ocean, she saw the third son of the great Water Dragon King. He was swimming through the waters in the form of a vast carp, on an errand for his father. As he did so, he unwittingly fell into the net of a fisherman who hauled him up and set off for the market. Miao

Shan, seeing his distress and predicament, sent Shan Tsai to the market with a vast fortune to purchase the carp. No sooner had Shan Tsai bought the fish than he took him to the sea and released him. When the son returned to his father, the Dragon King, he told him all that had happened. Deeply moved by this act of compassion, the great king ordered that Miao Shan be presented with a pearl of such luminosity that she would be able to read at night in the glow of its magic light.

When Lung Nu, the daughter of the Dragon King's third son, heard what had happened, she begged permission to take the pearl to Miao Shan and then to stay with her and study the scriptures and devotions of the Buddhist faith. She was granted permission and so Lung Nu came to Miao Shan, who was so taken by Lung Nu's sincerity that she asked her to stay with her and Shan Tsai. The two disciples of Miao Shan addressed each other as brother and sister and have remained by her side to this day.

Meanwhile, back in the palace the king's life went from bad to worse. Cursed by the gods for his bloody usurpation of the throne and by the Buddha for his treatment of Miao Shan, the king fell ill with a severe form of jaundice. His whole body was afflicted and broke into open sores. He was unable to sleep or rest, tossing and turning all day and all night. All the wisest doctors of the kingdom were summoned, but none could halt the spread and development of the disease. In desperation they tried every known cure but to no effect, for this was no ordinary ailment.

While he lay so ill, his two older daughters and their husbands feasted and rejoiced, believing that soon they would inherit the kingdom, and caring nothing for the distress of their poor father.

As the king lay at death's door, a strange monk suddenly appeared in the palace, claiming that he could cure the king. 'I have a divine remedy that will heal your majesty,' he said.

The king asked, 'What medicine do you have with you that can do this?'

The monk said, 'If you use the arm and eye of one who is without anger, combine them into a medicine and apply it, you will be cured.'

The king and his advisers were horrified by this. 'Where could I find such a person willing to make such a sacrifice for one like me?' asked the king.

The monk replied, 'On Pu To Shan you will find such a person. She is an immortal whose devotion to the Buddhist faith has brought her to the stage of perfection. She has no anger and will respond to your request.'

Immediately, the king ordered messengers to set out for the mountain to find this wonderful immortal and to beg for the ingredients of this terrible and strange prescription. The messengers were in the saddle and gone within minutes.

But all was not well in the palace. The two sons-in-law heard of the strange monk and feared lest the king recover and they lose their chance to reign. So they plotted together. They determined to poison the king that very night and to kill the monk so that the blame for the death of the king could be placed upon his shoulders. They intended to present the king with a broth which they would claim was the medicine prescribed by the monk. In this way they would deal with both king and monk. However, they were not alone. Lurking within the palace was the spirit on duty that day. Hearing this evil plan, he determined to foil them.

Later that evening, the two sons-in-law appeared in the king's bedroom bearing a bowl of poisoned soup. 'This is the medicine the monk has prescribed. Your august majesty, drink this marvellous elixir and be returned to full health,' they said. But before the king could lift the deadly brew to his lips, the door burst open and in rushed the spirit on duty that day. With a whirlwind he knocked the bowl to the floor and felled the two villains. Bowing before the king he explained the reason for his actions and the king, aghast at this treachery, had his two sons-in-law bound hand and foot and taken off to prison.

Meanwhile, elsewhere in the palace, the assassin selected by the sons-in-law crept into the room where the monk lay asleep. Raising his sword he brought it down upon the recumbent figure. But as the blade touched the robes of the monk, it became entangled. As the astonished murderer watched, the robes arose by themselves and wrapped themselves so tightly around the assassin that he could not move. But within the robes there was no body, for the monk had disappeared as mysteriously as he had arrived.

When the failed assassin was found the next day, he was tried and executed along with the two treacherous sons-in-law and it was only the frantic pleas of the queen which saved her two daughters.

While all this was unfolding at the palace, the messenger rode on through the day and night, arriving at the mountain at dawn. Finding Miao Shan, he knelt before her and delivered his message. She looked down and said 'My father has shown disrespect for the Three Great Treasures of the Buddhist faith. He has tried to suppress the Truth and has murdered innocent nuns. This should bring retribution.'

So saying she smiled upon the messenger, gouged out her eyes and cut off both arms, which she laid before the astonished and horrified messenger. As her offerings were gathered up, the whole earth shook at the momentousness of these actions. Before the messenger left Miao Shan said, 'Tell the king to turn from his evil ways and to embrace the True Path.'

When the messenger arrived back, he found the monk awaiting him by the palace gate. Handing over the gruesome trophies of his journey, the messenger went directly to the king to report his success. Moments later the monk strode into the king's chamber to the bewilderment of all. Speaking to the king, he handed over a mixture he had prepared of the gouged out eyes and truncated arms. Desperate, the king drank of the medical preparation without question, and instantly he was restored to full health. Falling on his knees, the king offered his thanks to the monk. But the monk dismissed this casually, saying, 'Why do you thank me? You should be thanking the one who gave her eyes and arms to heal you.' So saying he suddenly disappeared from their sight, never to be seen again.

The king and queen ordered their carriages to be made ready and with the whole court following, they set off that very day for the mountain. Arriving before the Bodhisattva, they bowed low and offered their thanks to the mutilated woman who stood before them. As the queen lifted her eyes to gaze upon the one who had saved her husband, she uttered a shriek of astonishment and horror, for she recognized that it was none other than her youngest daughter Miao Shan. The king, realizing what she had done for him despite all he had done to her, fell prostrate upon the floor and asked her forgiveness.

Miao Shan said, 'I am indeed Miao Shan. Mindful of my father's love, I have repaid him with my eyes and arms.'

Overcome with emotion, her parents embraced her and the king said, 'I am so evil that I have caused my daughter terrible suffering.'

Miao Shan replied, 'Father, I have suffered no pain. Having given up these human eyes, I shall see with diamond eyes. Having yielded up these mortal arms, I shall receive golden arms. If my vow is true, all this will follow.'

At these words, the mountain and indeed the whole world shook. Great clouds of many colours descended, a wonderful fragrance filled the air and divine flowers rained down everywhere, just as it had been at the birth of Miao Shan. When the clouds lifted, Miao Shan was revealed as the Thousand Armed and Thousand Eyed Kuan Yin. Hovering above her parents, she bade them return home and rule justly and fairly, following the precepts of Buddhism, the Buddhist faith. Then the Bodhisattva Kuan Yin, accompanied by Shan Ts'ai and Lung Nu, ascended into the clouds, the Bodhisattva radiating beauty like the Harvest Moon. Weeping, yet rejoicing at this revelation, the king and queen buried the mortal remains of their daughter and built a beautiful shrine over her body. Then, praising Kuan Yin, they returned to the palace and ruled for many years, teaching love and compassion and drawing the hearts of all in their kingdom into knowledge of the truth of the Buddhist faith. Indeed, it is said that at their deaths Heaven was seen to open and the merciful Kuan Yin welcome them into her divine home.

The tale of Monkey

The tale of Monkey is one of the best-known and most popular in Chinese folklore. It concerns the adventures of a motley group of travellers seeking to bring the Buddhist scriptures to China from the West. Nominally led by Sanzang, also known as Tripitaka, a holy Buddhist monk, the real leader is in fact Monkey, a macaque ape with vast magical powers.

It is Monkey's quick wit and sense of humour which really provides the heart of the stories. The obstacles encountered (normally demons and devils of various types, wishing to devour the holy Sanzang) are defeated not by brute force, but by Monkey's cunning tricks – normally delivered along with a little quip at the expense of his foe.

The humour of the stories is heightened by the presence of Pigsy. A heavenly government official banished for misbehaving himself, he has been incarnated into the womb of a pig, and is consequently hideously ugly. Not only that, but he is also lazy and stupid. The interaction between Monkey and Pigsy provides a great source of amusement – normally ending with Pigsy being humiliated in some way. Sanzang, the holy monk, is equally inept, being half wise man and half gullible fool.

The final members of this ill-matched group are Friar Sand, or Sandy, and the white horse. Friar Sand is another fallen heavenly official, incarnated this time into the body of a shark. He does not appear much in the tales, but when he does he provides a practical common sense which contrasts sharply with Monkey's tricks and Pigsy's buffoonery. The horse is a rebellious dragon who ate

Sanzang's original horse and has been transformed into equine shape as a punishment.

While this scruffy band may not seem to fit the roles of gods and heroes well, the rest of the deities are little better. The Jade Emperor, Heaven's ruler, is a weak, vacillating character who reigns over a court of sycophants, pompous clowns, and bureaucrats. The only truly admirable deities are the Buddhas and Bodhisattvas, who, as the story is told from a strongly Buddhist position, are always portrayed as powerful, wise, and kindly, especially Kuan Yin, the goddess of Mercy.

The story opens with the tale of Monkey's birth and how he acquires his powers...

Monkey Overthrows Heaven

Once there lived a monkey. This was no ordinary monkey, for he had been formed near the beginning of the universe and cracked out of a primordial stone. His eyes shone like jacinths, and when he smiled his teeth reflected the light of the stars. His body was supernaturally tough, and his strength was great. Being a monkey, he was also extremely cunning, even if he lacked any sense of decorum. Naturally, he took over all the rest of his tribe, calling himself simply 'Monkey'.

Eventually, after ruling the apes, monkeys, gorillas and so on for over a hundred years, he grew bored, and set off to seek wisdom. On his long and arduous journeying, he learned great mystic powers, such as the ability to transform into different shapes, many magic spells, and the art of travelling on a cloud. Not only this, but he could create a hundred thousand duplicates of himself simply by plucking out a handful of his hairs and shouting 'Change!'. He also swindled a Dragon King out of a great magic

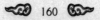

staff which could change to any size, from a pillar capable of touching Heaven to a tiny needle which Monkey kept neatly tucked behind his ear. With his new powers he subdued all the demons on his home kingdom, making the greatest of them into his generals.

Armed with this arsenal of magical equipment, Monkey leapt up to Heaven and demanded to be given a position. The Jade Emperor, cowardly ruler of Heaven, was terrified by this frightening apparition, but his wise advisors gave Monkey a minor position – Protector of the Horses. Monkey eventually found out how unimportant this post was, and raised great havoc in Heaven, wrecking the Halls of Miraculous Mist and defeating many warriors in single combat. Eventually he was given the title 'Great Sage Equalling Heaven' and, to keep him quiet, he was put in charge of looking after the Peach Orchard in Heaven.

The first day Monkey went to take up his post he was awestruck by the sheer size and beauty of the Peach Garden. It stretched as far as he could see, and every tree was laden down with fruit. Despite it being winter down on Earth, the Garden was warm and calm. It never rained, but a rainbow was eternally stretched across the sky. Impressed by the magnificence of the Garden, Monkey called the gardeners to him and asked about the powers of the peaches. The gardener gods pointed out various peaches to him. 'You see those ones at the front, the small ones? You only get those once every three thousand years. If anybody eats those, he becomes Immortal. The ones in the middle ripen every six thousand years, and with those you can enjoy eternal youth and soar into the sky at will. The back ones are streaked with purple – a bit unusual for peaches, but these are Heavenly peaches, after all. One bite of those will make you eternal as Heaven and Earth, and you will stay healthy as long as the Sun and Moon remain in the sky.'

Monkey already had all of these powers and more, but he was still filled with a desire to eat some of the peaches. After a few days, when all the peaches were nearly ripe, he sent the gardener gods away, claiming he was about to take a nap in the summer-house. He gorged himself on the purple-streaked peaches, then settled down in the trees and began to take a nap.

On that day, however, the Queen Mother was holding a banquet in Heaven, and had sent along seven of her spirits to go and pick some peaches for her. They picked many basketfuls of the peaches at the front, and even more basketfuls of the ones in the middle, but when they came to the trees at the back, they saw to their astonishment that all the peaches, except for a few unripe ones, had been eaten. One of the spirits shook a tree to try and see if any were left along the branches, and the Great Sage was woken abruptly. Leaping down, Monkey produced his gold-banded cudgel and shook it threateningly. 'Who are you, you thieves?' he shouted furiously. The spirits cowered back in terror. 'Please Great Sage, don't hit us with your cudgel. We are no thieves, but attendant spirits sent by the Queen Mother to pick peaches for her banquet.' Monkey stared at them with his fierce green eyes. 'Who's invited to this banquet, then?' he snarled. The spirits began to reel off a list of heavenly deities. 'Stop, stop!' said Monkey, 'What I mean is, am I invited?' 'No – I mean, not that we know of, Great Sage Equalling Heaven,' said one of the spirits, nervously eyeing Monkey's wavering cudgel. 'Huh,' said Monkey, 'I'll just go and correct that little mistake.'

Splendid Monkey leapt onto his cloud and headed towards the Heavenly Palace. Below him he saw the Bare-foot Immortal, clearly heading towards the banquet. He hailed the Immortal. 'Venerable Sir, you are heading in the wrong direction,' he shouted. 'An opening ceremony is being held in the Hall of Universal Brightness, and we must all go in there first.' The trusting Immortal immediately turned around and began heading towards the Hall. Meanwhile Monkey landed his cloud, transformed himself into the Bare-foot Immortal, and casually strode into the banquet.

None of the other guests had yet arrived, but the banquet was all laid out. All kinds of wondrous foods, such as dragon livers and the bones of the phoenix, were spread over the table. What most caught Monkey's eye were the large jars of liquor. Drooling, he sent the servants to sleep with a simple spell, grabbed several of the choice items, and went over to drain the jars. Once he was completely drunk, he suddenly thought 'Oh Way, what happens if they catch me here? I'm for it then.' Staggering out of the doors and knocking over a couple of tables, he attempted to make his way back to his house. However he was so completely drunk he found himself instead at the residence of Lord Lao Zi. Intending to go and have a friendly chat with Lord Lao Zi, he found he was out, lecturing to the Jade Emperor's court. However, his greedy eye fell on some of the golden pills of Lao Zi. 'Wonderful,' he thought. 'These grant great endurance to the eater. I've always meant to come along and ask for some, but since he's out I'm sure he won't mind if I take a few.' Monkey began to chomp down the pills as though they were beans. Before long he was completely sober, and in a state of utter terror at the thought of all he had done. He quietly sneaked out of Heaven, and made his way back down to his people, where he found them practising their drill. He ordered a banquet to celebrate his return, and even crept back into Heaven to steal several jars of immortal wine. Soon all the monkeys and demons were very happy indeed that their ruler had returned.

While all this was going on, the Jade Emperor had been informed of the theft of the Golden Pills, the eating of the Heavenly Peaches, and the wrecking of his mother-in-law's banquet. Aided by the testimony of the Bare-foot Immortal and the seven attendant spirits, he soon identified the culprit and flew into a great rage. 'Send a hundred thousand heavenly soldiers down to catch that wretch,' he yelled, 'and we will have him slaughtered for his impertinence.' Immediately a huge army of soldiers was sent down, accompanied by several Immortals. They pitched camp before the Mountain of Flowers and Fruit, where Monkey was holding his banquet. Monkey ordered his own forces out of the cave in which they were feasting, and a great melee ensued.

With his massive cudgel Monkey himself personally saw off the Four Heavenly Kings, Prince Nezha, and the Nine Bright Shiners, all powerful immortals, while the battle raged in the heavens. Now a thousand monkeys rushed against the flank of the soldiers, then a rain of crossbow quarrels came down on them, and they were forced to retreat until one of the demon generals rushed forward to aid them. The demon kings stormed into the centre of the melee, laying blows all around them. Animals fled in terror and no bird would approach as the battle raged ferociously on. Monkey was getting tired at this point, so he tore out a handful of his hairs, yelled 'Charge!', and a thousand Great Sages, all with gold-banded cudgels, charged the foe, who were forced to retreat in terror.

When Monkey called his forces before him, he saw that though many Heavenly soldiers had been killed, his demon generals had all been captured. His forces were in despair, and so Monkey bellowed out 'Don't worry, little ones. We'll retake our friends and avenge our fallen brothers. Things like this must happen in war. But we'll do all this tomorrow, for tonight we must rest and eat our fill or we won't stand a chance.' When they heard this speech the monkeys all kowtowed before their wise leader, and went to their beds.

When he heard of the defeat of his army, the Jade Emperor was in despair. In desperation, he sent for merciful Kuan Yin and asked the Bodhisattva if she had a solution. Now Kuan Yin, in her great wisdom, knew that Monkey had a greater role to play than this, but she also knew that he must first be captured and subdued. She lent the Jade Emperor her disciple Huian, also known as Prince Moksha, the second son of Heavenly Lord Li, who had considerable powers. The Jade Emperor ordered him down to the Mountain of Flowers and Fruit.

Despite his years of tuition under the Bodhisattva, Prince Moksha was a cocky sort. He strode confidently up to the doors of Monkey's cave, followed by two hundred thousand Heavenly soldiers, and rapped confidently. Monkey stuck his head out. 'Go away!' he shouted. 'I'm trying to sleep!'

Huian replied in an arrogant voice, 'I am Prince Moksha, the second son of Heavenly Lord Li, and I have been sent to capture you, you foolish ape.'

'You talk big, don't you?' answered Monkey. 'Let's see how well you can take a blow from my cudgel.'

Immediately Moksha struck at Monkey with his iron staff, and the two Immortals leapt into the sky, engaging in fearsome combat. Below them the Heavenly soldiers rushed against Monkey's forces, and battle ensued again, even more ferocious than before.

Prince Moksha was a skilled fighter and wielded his Heaven-forged staff well, making quick attacks against Monkey and parrying Monkey's swift replies, but Monkey had considerably more endurance. After about sixty rounds, and after parrying thousands of Monkey's lightning-quick strikes with his deadly cudgel, Huian's arm was aching, and he felt so tired he could hardly lift his staff anymore. Feinting to distract Monkey's attention, he turned and fled, while Monkey shouted curses and insults at his rapidly retreating back. Exhausted, Moksha sped up to Heaven where he reported his defeat. The Jade Emperor tore at his hair. 'This accursed ape has enough tricks to defeat anyone!' he screamed, ranting and raving around his palace. Once he had calmed down, Guanyin quietly made a suggestion:

'Your Majesty, have you thought of trying your nephew Erlang? He has many powers and has defeated several horrible monsters and fiends in the past. Send a messenger to him.' The Jade Emperor took her advice and sent off a speedy messenger to deliver a letter begging for his nephew's help.

Erlang was greatly pleased to receive such a fine challenge, and sped over to the Mountain of Flower and Fruit, where he immediately challenged the tired Monkey to combat. Monkey spat back at him, cursing his name, and swung his cudgel at his head. Erlang caught the blow with his iron staff, and swiftly struck back at Monkey. So began their ferocious combat. The blows fell thick and fast, and each knew that a single blow from the other's staff could crush their heads like a ripe melon, but after three hundred rounds the victor was still undecided. Erlang paused for a moment, and by merely shaking his body became ten thousand fathoms tall. Clutching a two-bladed trident, and with a black face, fire-red hair and mile-long fangs, he looked terrifying. Monkey merely laughed and, also resorting to magic, made his own body as tall as Erlang's and his face as monstrous. In his hands his gold-banded cudgel swelled to the size of one of the great pillars of Heaven, and the two great Immortals together blotted out the sun. Their combat started up again. Each step to the side shook the land, and each missed blow could swipe the top of a mountain. Luckily for the world, they had only fought a few rounds when Monkey noticed that on the ground, his forces were losing badly. With no stomach for the fight anymore, Monkey turned tail and fled.

Seeing that Erlang was hot on his tail, Monkey made a quick gesture and vanished. Erlang stopped and opened his magical phoenix eyes, looking around for the treacherous macaque. Seeing that Monkey had transformed into a sparrow and was sitting chirping on a branch, he put off his magical appearance, dropped his trident, and changed himself into a kite. Monkey, panicking, flew off the branch and changed into a cormorant, quickly flapping off into the sky. Erlang saw him, and with a quick twist of his avian body and a hunting cry, he changed into a white-feathered crane and chased after Monkey. Monkey landed by a mountain stream and swiftly changed into a fish, plunging into the cold water. Erlang, realizing that Monkey must have become some kind of fish, transformed into a fish-hawk and began to fly over the stream. When he spotted a fish that turned round nervously when it saw him, he dived down and snapped at Monkey, who only just escaped by leaping out of the water and transmuting himself into a river-snake. Erlang gave a fearsome cry and leapt after him, becoming a red-crested grey crane as he did so, attempting to catch Monkey in his long beak. Monkey flicked away and changed into a bustard, perching on a weed-covered bank. Frustrated, Erlang reverted to his own form, and, pulling out his magical crossbow, knocked Monkey head over heels with only one shot.

As Monkey rolled down the precipice he grabbed on to a rock and pulled himself onto a crag, seizing the chance to transform himself into a temple to a local deity. He opened his mouth wide to resemble the entrance, and turned his teeth into the doors; his tongue became the god's statue and his eyes two large windows. He stuck his tail up straight behind him as a flagpole. When Erlang came to the precipice and peered down he could not see the bustard he had knocked over, but spotting the temple, thought to himself 'That must be the treacherous ape! I've seen many temples, but never one with a flagpole at the back before.' Seeing Erlang bear down on him Monkey gave a great tiger leap and vanished into the sky.

Erlang looked around but was unable to see Monkey. Asking one of his generals to consult his magic fiend-detecting mirror, he saw with a shock that Monkey had leapt over to his own palace. Rushing over there, he found Monkey transformed into his own image, inspecting the offerings and the intercessions; pork presented by a Li Hu, a prayer from a Zhao Jia asking for fertility, and one Qian Bing's prayer to be relieved from his illness. When Erlang arrived Monkey reverted to his own form and shouted 'Go away, you pompous fool. This temple's mine now, and there's no point in trying to prove otherwise.' The True Lord gave no answer, but swung his double-bladed trident straight at Monkey's head. Monkey nimbly evaded the blow and drew out his own cudgel, giving a great howl and thrusting with his cudgel at Erlang's head.

Well, they fought many rounds, up and down the length of China, and Erlang called on all his generals to come and aid him, but they were unable to contain the Monkey King, who fought like a wildcat, striking here, striking there, and with never a gap in his defences. Up in Heaven the Bodhisattva Kuan Yin said to Lao Zi, 'What do you think of that god I recommended? He's certainly got Monkey cornered. Will you be a dear and just drop this vase on his head so they can finally overwhelm him?' Lao Zi took the vase, and, baking it in his Eight Trigrams furnace in which he brewed his elixir, made it hard as steel. He tossed it out of the gates of Heaven, whereby it fell to Earth, falling with a bump on Monkey's head and laying him spread-eagled. Erlang and his generals fell on him and bound him tightly, then the True Lord lifted him up to Heaven.

After Erlang had been praised for his skill and valour in subduing the ape, Monkey was taken out and tied to a pillar. There they tried all manner of things to kill him. They hacked at him with great axes, sliced him with swords, lunged at him with spears, but all of it did not harm a single one of Monkey's hairs. Frustrated, all the gods of Fire tried to ignite him, but Monkey merely complained about the unpleasant warmth. He was punched, kicked, had lightning thrown at him, was burnt, stabbed – all the many deaths were tried on him, but nothing had any effect, as he was so hardened from the peaches of immortality, the imperial liquor and the pills of immortality. His own evil crimes were protecting him.

Eventually, in frustration, Lao Zi ordered him baked in his own Eight Trigrams furnace, which would melt him down and allow his precious elixir to be retrieved. Now, this furnace consisted of Eight Trigrams – Qian, Kan, Gen, Zhen, Sun, Li, Kun, and Dui – so the ingenious Monkey squeezed himself into the Sun, or wind, Trigram, where the wind blew the fire out. All that was produced was a huge amount of smoke, which made both Monkey's eyes red and watery. Eventually, Lord Lao Zi thought his body would have been refined down to its base elements by this point, and opened the furnace. Monkey, busy rubbing his eyes, saw the daylight and leapt out, headbutting Lord Lao Zi, who staggered back, clutching at his face. He saw the furnace and kicked it over with an almighty crash, and was off. He was like an unleashed tiger or a raging tornado, rushing through the Heavenly Palace and wrecking everything in his path. Nobody could restrain him; he kicked the Kingly Spirit Officer in the groin, sent Lord Nezha flying head over heels, and stamped on the Bare-foot Immortal's toes. Soon many of the halls and palaces of Heaven were reduced to rubble, and all the thirty-six thunder generals were sent to subdue him. Monkey gave a fiendish laugh, and, whirling round, grew six arms and three heads. Then he shook his cudgel and changed it into three cudgels. Clutching his new weaponry, he began to spin round and round, creating a deadly circle of devastation. None of the gods could get near enough to harm him, and arrows glanced off his body, refined and hardened by the Eight Trigrams furnace. He seemed almost invincible.

In desperation, the Jade Emperor sent for the Buddha Tathagata himself. Arriving at the courts, the Buddha landed his cloud and dismissed the thunder generals. Monkey stopped spinning, and, said, panting, 'What's with you? You come along and ruin a perfectly good fight – what a nerve!'

'I am the Venerable Buddha,' said the Buddha, smiling. 'I have been informed of your insolent and boorish behaviour, and I want to know on what grounds you have the right to the heavenly throne?' Monkey began to reel off a list of his many powers; riding on clouds, transformations, immortality, jumping thirty-six thousand miles in one leap – the list went on and on. 'Alright, alright,' said the Buddha, 'I'll make a bet with you. I bet you can't even leap out of the palm of my hand, you dastardly ape. If you make it, then I'll invite the Jade Emperor to come and live with me, and you can have these palaces. But if you fail...' He left the threat hanging in the air.

Monkey thought, 'What an idiot. I've just told him I can leap thirty-six thousand miles with a somersault, so why does he challenge me to this, when his palm is less than a foot across. Ah well, never give a sucker an even break.'

With this thought Monkey leapt onto the Buddha's hand, then twirled off again, going like a streak of light from the sun himself. Whirling round and round in the air and not stopping, he saw five huge pink pillars topped by dark vapours. 'The pillars which hold up the sky!' he thought. 'I'll write my name here, and that'll prove I've won.' Monkey yanked out a hair and transformed it into a writing-brush, then quickly wrote 'The Great Sage Equalling Heaven Was Here,' on the middle pillar, in large letters. Burping, he realized he had not had a chance to go to the toilet since he had downed the heavenly liquor, so he pissed all over the middle pillar. He then leaped back to the Buddha.

'I've won!' he yelled.

'You piss-poor spirit of an ape,' the Buddha laughed. 'You never left my hand!'

Monkey indignantly said, 'What! I leapt to the furthest point of Heaven, wrote my name on one of the pillars that hold up the sky, and had a piss! Do you want to come and have a look, laughing boy?'

The Buddha silently held out his hand, and peering with his fire eyes Monkey saw the words 'The Great Sage Equalling Heaven Was Here' written on the middle finger. The stench of his piss rose from the folds at the bottom. Monkey staggered back in amazement. 'He must be cheating and using divination to know what I would do, then changed his hand,' he thought, and attempted to leap off to go and check the pillars. Before he could do so, the Buddha put his five fingers together and Monkey found himself beneath a mountain range on Earth, only his head protruding, and the weight of the mountain bearing down on his aching back.

The Buddha had a merciful heart, and knew of the role that Monkey was going to play in the journey to the West, and so instructed the local deities to keep guard over him. When he was hungry they fed him copper pellets, and when he was thirsty he was given molten bronze to drink. And there he remained, in terrible pain, for many, many thousands of years.

After being put under the mountain, Monkey remains there for thousands of years. Fortunately, he is eventually rescued by the divinely inspired Sanzang, on his way to India to obtain Buddhist holy scriptures and relics. They travel along together, but in order to restrain Monkey's natural violence the Goddess Kuan Yin puts a band around his head which, whenever Sanzang recites a magic formula, tightens, giving Monkey an appalling migraine.

They also pick up the dragon, who having devoured Sanzang's horse is transformed into a white stallion as punishment, and Pigsy. Pigsy, following his natural character, is engaging in a life of

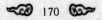

debauchery, terrorising villages with his powers in return for food, wine, and women. Monkey is easily able to overcome him, and he joins the group in penance. Much the same occurs with Sandy, who is waylaying and murdering travellers.

After many adventures, including such exploits as the restoration of a murdered prince and the foiling of many demons' attempts to devour Sanzang, they eventually arrive in the land of Tarrycart, which is where our next story takes place.

Monkey and the Demon Taoists

As the four friends wandered along, enjoying the signs of new life and relaxing after a harsh and snow-battered journey, they came upon a most unusual and unpleasant sight. As they crested a hill, they saw a valley filled with a huge crowd of Buddhist monks. Though no vastly unusual sight, what did seem odd was that they were all engaged in various menial tasks – pulling carts, laying bricks, and hammering wood.

Though at first the companions merely assumed the monks were building a monastery, Monkey began to get a little suspicious when he noticed the arrival of two foppishly dressed Taoist priests, their elaborate robes and sparkling jewellery a stark contrast to the rags of the monks. At the arrival of the priests, all the monks started to quake in fear and began sawing, pulling, or laying with renewed vigour – vigour Monkey feared arose out of terror of punishment. Curious, he clapped his hands and took on the liking of a wandering Taoist monk. While the others waited, Monkey strode forward, beating on his wooden hand drum and chanting Taoist songs as he went.

Monkey knelt down before the two Taoists, trying hard to conceal a smirk as he said 'Humblest greetings, elders in the Way.'

One of the Taoists looked haughtily down at the poor-seeming Monkey and replied 'Where are you from, stranger, and what business do you have in this town?'

Monkey answered 'I'm from all around the place, and I seek only to find a bit of food to eat. Where's the best street to beg round here, brothers?'

At this the priests burst out laughing. 'Beg! He thinks you have to beg to get your food round here! My dear sir, in the kingdom of Tarrycart, all of us, from the lowliest street urchin to the highest general, love and follow the Way. People will be pressing food upon you as soon as you step within these gates. After all, the king is extremely fond of us Taoists.'

On hearing this Monkey replied, smiling, 'By any wild chance is a Taoist priest the monarch?'

'Oh no,' replied the priest, 'It's just that for many years we had a terrible, earth-scorching drought here, and nothing could grow. Everyone prayed, bathed, and invoked heaven, from the king downwards. When things got really desperate, three Immortals were sent down from Heaven to aid us – the Great Immortals Tiger Power, Deer Power, and Antelope Power. They have great and wonderful magic powers, and caused the rain to fall. Our king treats them with great respect, and all Taoist priests with them.'

'What about the Buddhist monks working there?' inquired Monkey.

'Surely, as fellow men of religion, they ought to be treated as well as us?'

'Ah, but what you don't know,' retorted the priest, 'is that these so-called monks couldn't get a single drop of rain to fall! All their invoking the Buddha and chanting sutras had no effect whatsoever! Consequently, our king was so angry that, on the Immortals' suggestion, he had their temples burnt down, their statues smashed, and gave them all to us Taoists as slaves, to build our new residence. We arrest any of them who try to get away. You can normally recognize them by the chanting and the bald heads. There have been a few problems with people who weren't actually

172

Buddhists, just a little thin on top, but that's all been sorted out. And now that they're slaves, all we have to feed them is one bowl of rice a day. Wonderful, isn't it?'

Cunning Monkey immediately fell to his knees. 'My brothers, what a coincidence! I am looking for an uncle of mine who joined the Buddhists a while back. Now you have them gathered all in one place, it will be much, much easier to find him. Do you mind if I go over and have a look?'

'Not at all,' replied the priest, 'And if you find him, bring him back here, and, seeing as you're a fellow Taoist, we'll free him.'

As soon as Monkey wandered over, all the monks fell to their knees. 'Get up, get up,' said Monkey, 'I'm not really a Taoist priest.'

'Who are you then, Master?' asked one of the monks.

'That doesn't matter. What matters is that I'm here to set you free.'

'Master, by any chance is your name the Great Sage of the East?'

'Why, yes,' answered Monkey. 'How did you know?'

The monk replied, 'Every night, when we fall asleep, we see spirits before us. They reassure us, saying "Don't worry. A Great Sage will soon come from the East to free you. He has immense magical powers, is immensely wise, has a good and loyal heart, he rights wrongs, he saves those in distress, and he helps widows and orphans. He will defeat the Taoists and restore the faith to its rightful position." For many of us, this reassurance is the only thing keeping us alive.'

On hearing this, Monkey said with a chuckle, 'And about my modesty they say nothing? Typical, typical. Now you lot just wait here and I'll go and deal with that pair of priests over there.'

While the monks waited, Monkey strolled back to the priests. 'Which one was your uncle?' they asked.

'All of them are my relations,' Monkey jovially answered.

'All of them!' gasped the startled priests.

'Yes, all,' said Monkey, 'Some of them lived to my right, some of them lived to my left, a hundred are my father's kin, two hundred are my mothers, twenty went to school with me, fifteen...'

'Enough, enough!' shouted the priest, 'Even if they are all your relations, we can't let them all go. We'd be in terrible trouble. Outrageous, quite outrageous.'

At this Monkey's temper snapped, and he drew his cudgel and smote the priests a mighty blow. The two Taoists fell to the ground stone-dead, and the monks came running up, imploring Monkey. 'Great Sage, what are we to do now? Those two priests were the king's relations. Now, if they catch us, we won't just be imprisoned, we'll be killed.'

'Don't worry, I'll give you protection.' said Monkey, drawing out a handful of his hairs and giving one to each monk. 'Put these under your fingernails. Now, shout out "Great Sage Equalling Heaven!"' As the monks did this, over each of them appeared a terrifying thunder god, his face snarling and holding a huge cudgel, frightening enough to scare off a whole army. 'That ought to protect you,' said Monkey. 'Shout "Quiet!" to make them go back under your nails. Now, when you see a proclamation recalling Buddhist monks, come to the city and give me my hair back. For the moment, scatter, though I want some of you to take my master, Sanzang, and get him some food and shelter. My friends and I are going to go and deal with the Taoists.'

Some of the monks led Sanzang and the horse off, while Monkey found Pigsy and Sandy. Quickly telling them of the situation in the city, they began to make their way into the city on their clouds. Peering down from above, they saw the lamps and candles of a large temple, and, when they brought their clouds lower for a better look, saw that the Taoists were performing a ritual. About eight hundred Taoist priests were clapping, banging hand-drums, swinging bells and burning incense. At the front were three wizened old men wearing Taoist robes, who Monkey assumed to be the three so-called Great Immortals.

Laid out before the altar in the temple was food of all types; cakes, steamed buns, rice, and huge amounts of fresh fruit. The smell of all this food made Pigsy's stomach rumble, and he was just about to lunge forward, heedless of all the Taoists, and begin

stuffing his mouth, when Monkey caught him with a muttered warn-
ing, 'Hold back, Brother Pigsy. We'll eat our share once they're gone.'

'But they've only just started,' moaned Pigsy. 'They'll be ages
yet, and I haven't eaten for hours.'

'Don't worry for your stomach, Pigsy. I'll do some magic that'll
get them away at once,' replied Monkey, drawing in a huge breath
and puffing out his cheeks.

'What are you going to do?' laughed Pigsy. 'Scare them away
with your bad breath?'

Monkey took no heed of the idiot but instead blew out his
breath, making the gestures of a spell at the same time. Immediately a terrible wind swept round the temple, knocking over the
vases, candles and offerings, and blowing out the smoking
incense and the lamps. The Taoists were all shivering with fear and
it took only a brief mention of bad omens from the Great Immortal
Tiger Power to make them all scarper back to their rooms.

Monkey, Pigsy, and Sandy landed their clouds and charged
straight into the temple. Pigsy was about to begin gobbling the
food when Monkey caught him again. 'Brother Pigsy,' he said,
'There are still a few more things we must do to make ourselves
safe. You see those statues of the Three Pure Ones on the altar?
We must turn ourselves into those as a disguise.'

Pigsy was ravenous, so he clambered onto the altar and
knocked the statues to the ground. Once they had transformed
themselves and were in the place of the statues, Pigsy grabbed a
large cake. This time it was Sandy who restrained him. 'Hold on a
minute, Pigsy. What if the Taoists come in here and see those statues on the floor? The game's up then, isn't it.'

'Good point,' said Monkey thoughtfully. 'When we came in,
there was a little pair of doors with a terrible stink coming from
behind them. As the Taoists would say, it must be the place where
grain prepares itself for reincarnation. Go and dump them in there.'

Pigsy heaved all three of the statues over his broad shoulders
and carried them to the double doors. Kicking the doors down he
discovered it was in fact a large lavatory. 'Monkey certainly knows

how the Taoists think!' he laughed, 'He's even come up with a fancy Taoist name for the toilet.' Before throwing the statues in, he knelt in mock piety and mumbled a prayer.

'Three Pure Ones, hear my prayer. We have come from a far away land to recover the scriptures, and, understandably, we're more than a bit hungry. Now, you're no doubt sitting up in heaven stuffing yourselves with nectar and peaches, so you won't mind if we eat these offerings. We've also had to borrow your pedestals, as there's nowhere else to sit. Normally, I'm sure you're pure and devout Taoists. However, today you're going to have to taste some filth and be the Three Pure but Stinking Ones.'

His duty done, Pigsy heaved the statues into the cesspit and went back to the other two. They then began to munch down the food, starting with the steamed bread and then going on to wolf down anything they could get their hands on. When the three friends had finished, the hall was covered in crumbs, bits of rice, and fruit stones. Rather than leave, they stayed to chat and slowly digest the gargantuan meal.

It was at this point that a young Taoist, who had left his handbell behind in the rush to get out of the temple earlier, came back to retrieve it. He had just found it when he heard the sound of breathing, and, in alarm, rushed out of the temple. On the way he slipped on a lychee stone and his bell shattered into a thousand pieces. Pigsy let out a great laugh at the boy's misfortune, which terrified the poor Taoist out of his wits. He ran out of the temple, screaming about evil creatures and demons. Hearing this, all the Taoists awoke, and, led by the three Great Immortals, ran to the temple to see what was going on.

As the Taoists rushed in all three of the impostors froze where they were, trying to look like statues. Monkey was picking his teeth, Pigsy still had half a steamed bun crammed in his mouth, and Sandy was in the middle of telling a joke, with his mouth wide open. The Taoists didn't spot them at first as they were still shaded by the darkness, until, having searched the whole temple and found no evil demons or spirits, they decided to check the statues hadn't been damaged. Great Immortal Tiger Power lifted up his lamp to the statues and leapt back in surprise. 'Look, brothers,' he yelled. 'The Great Immortals themselves have been moved by our prayers and invocations and have come down from Heaven to eat our offerings!'

Immediately all of the Taoists fell to their knees and kowtowed before the 'Three Pure Ones'. The Great Immortal Deer Power then prayed to the 'Pure Ones'.

'Oh Great Pure Ones, we are three humble Taoists who have been attempting to spread the Way in this city. We have suppressed the Buddhists' low vulgarity and have built many new temples in your honour. We worship with the uttermost sincerity and devotion. Now you have honoured us with your august presence, grant us some tablets of golden elixir and holy water to prolong the life of our most noble and devout king.'

Monkey immediately opened his mouth and called out in a deep, booming voice. 'Young immortals, I'm afraid we've just come from a Peach Banquet, so we clean forgot to bring any golden pills or holy water. We'll bring you some another day.'

All the Taoists gathered round the Great Immortals, saying, 'My lords, this is the only chance we'll ever get. Don't let them go till they give us a little holy water.'

At this the Great Immortal Deer Power kowtowed again, further reciting their advancement of Taoism and imploring Monkey to grant them some holy water. Monkey spoke again. 'Young immortals and devout followers of the Way, we weren't certain at first of your devotion, but we see you are clearly sincere. Fetch us some jars and we will give you some holy water.'

Several of the Taoists scampered out and came back with some large jars. 'Now,' said Monkey, 'leave the room while we prepare some holy water. The secrets of Heaven must not be revealed.' The Taoists kowtowed in thanks and immediately left the Temple, waiting outside in eager anticipation.

'Brother Monkey, you've really dropped us in it this time,' said Sandy. 'Where on earth are we going to get holy water? We better nip out the back door quickly.'

In reply, Monkey lifted up his loincloth and filled one of the jars with stinking piss. The other two caught on fast and immediately filled the other jars. They then rearranged their clothing, sat down, and called out 'Come and receive the holy water.'

The three Great Immortals hurried back in again and kowtowed in gratitude. One of the younger Taoists fetched a cup and Tiger Power filled the cup with the 'holy water', downed it, and made a great show of licking and smacking his lips.

'Is it good?' asked Deer Power. Tiger Power whispered in a barely audible monotone 'Not terribly. Tastes a little bit sour.'

'Let me have a sip,' said Antelope Power. He drained the cup and said 'Tastes rather like pig's urine.'

On hearing this Monkey decided that the game was up and yelled out 'You foolish Taoists! What utter rubbish you imagine. We're not the Three Pure Ones, we're Buddhist monks from the Great Tang, travelling west to receive the scriptures. We'd just finished this fine meal when you came in and started up with all your chanting nonsense. What you've been drinking isn't holy water – it's our piss!'

The Taoists immediately flew into a rage and surged forward to grab the miscreants. The three friends huddled together and charged through the crowd, leaping onto their clouds and flying back to the monastery where Sanzang had been taken. There they slept off their fine meal – especially the wine.

The next day, Sanzang decided to go to the king and ask for an exit permit. His three disciples accompanied him, a little shamefaced at their exploits of the day before. They were escorted into a waiting room, having told the guard of their purpose, while the king consulted with his advisors. Though they were Buddhist monks, the king decided, in the cause of good diplomatic relations with China, to grant them their exit permits. They were just about to have their passports stamped when, with a sinking heart, Monkey saw the three Taoists enter and rush forwards to the king.

'Your Majesty, you cannot let these criminals leave. Last night the three shady looking ones broke into the temple of the Three

Pure Ones and stole their offerings. Not only that, but your two relations who were guarding the Buddhists at the gate have been killed, and the monks released. It can only be these slimy foreigners who have done it,' said Antelope Power.

The king grew red in the face with anger and was about to order the execution of our four heroes when quick-witted Monkey stepped forward. 'Your Majesty, do these priests have any proof of these crimes? We would never commit such foul deeds – we are all good and honest monks. I think they're trying to frame us.'

'The dull-witted king did not know what to make of this, and he was racked with indecision. At this point a eunuch came forward to report, 'Your Majesty, there is a group of elders outside waiting to speak to you. There has been no rain this spring and they fear a drought. What shall I tell them?'

The king replied 'Tell them there will be rain.' The eunuch kowtowed and withdrew, and the king turned to Sanzang. 'I have decided on a way to settle this argument. You will go and have a rain-making competition with the revered Teachers of the Nation. If you win, you may go. If you lose, I will have you publicly executed.'

'We humble monks know a little about rain-making,' said Monkey with a smile.

The rain-making ritual took place at the bottom of a huge tower, from which the king watched. Tiger Power stepped forward. 'Your Majesty,' he said, 'when I wave my wand this first time the winds will blow, the second time the clouds will rise, the third time thunder will sound and lightning will flash across the sky, the fourth time it will rain, and, upon the last wave, the rain will stop and the clouds disperse.'

'Splendid,' said Monkey. 'What amazing powers you Taoists have. Go ahead.'

The Immortal began his ritual surrounded by all manner of ceremonial paraphernalia. He chanted Taoist hymns, broke open wax figures, had other priests bang drums, and then waved his wand once. Immediately a huge wind sprang up. 'This is bad,' muttered Pigsy.

'This is really bad. It looks like the Taoists do have some powers.'
'Wait here,' said Monkey, 'and I'll see what I can do.'

The Great Sage immediately plucked out another hair and turned it into an imitation Monkey, which sat there patiently while the real Monkey leaped into the air just as the wand was waved a second time and the clouds began to spread out. In the air were all manner of supernatural beings; Granny Wind with her magic bag, Boy Cloudspreader and Lord Mistspreader shoving out the clouds, and, waiting to perform their role, the thunder and lightning gods, and the four dragon kings in charge of the winds. 'What's going on here?' bellowed Monkey. The dragon king Ao Guang came forward and humbly kowtowed before Monkey. 'Great Sage,' he said. 'The Taoist has filled out an application to the heavenly courts for all the necessary deities to make rain. We have been commanded to aid him.'

'Right,' said Monkey. 'Listen here, all you lot. Most of you know me of old and half of you owe me favours. Now, out of friendship, I'll give you one chance to stop all of this before I give you all twenty strokes of my Heaven-Defeating cudgel.' The assorted gods quaked in fear of Monkey.

On the ground the Taoists saw the wind drop and the clouds roll back. In panic, Tiger Power began chanting furiously, waving his wand around and ordering more incense to be burnt – but nothing happened. Eventually he was forced to step down. Monkey immediately whispered to the gods, 'Right. My master is going to pray now. I'm going to use my cudgel to give orders.'

The gods reeled back in shock. 'But Great Sage, none of us can take one blow of your cudgel,' exclaimed Granny Wind.

'I'm not going to hit you with it – unless you make any mistakes,' said Monkey. 'When I raise it once, I want wind, the second time clouds, the third thunder and lightning, the fourth rain, and the fifth time the rain must stop. Got it?' The gods nodded fearfully.

On the ground Sanzang calmly stepped forwards. He knew he didn't have any magic powers, and Monkey, to his eyes, didn't seem to be doing anything, but he was determined to have the best try he could. He made his way with great dignity to the altar, sat down in the lotus position, and quietly began to recite the Heart Sutra. Monkey immediately raised his cudgel once, and a great wind began to whip across the landscape. He raised it twice, and black clouds rolled in from all four quarters of the earth. He raised it for the third time, and lightning streaked across the sky as a great boom of thunder sounded. Back on the earth the Taoists were muttering oaths as the king, along with all of the common people and courtiers, were gazing open-mouthed at the sky. As the storm built to a climax, Monkey raised the cudgel again, and a heavy rain began to fall.

It was an incredible deluge. The gods, in fear of Monkey's cudgel, had pulled all the stops out. The rivers began to swell, the rice fields were almost turning into miniature oceans, and dry land was swallowed up by water in an instant. After about an hour, the streets of Tarrycart were flowing with water and the king humbly asked Sanzang to stop, or the whole kingdom would be drowned. Sanzang immediately stopped chanting, and Monkey raised his cudgel a last time. Immediately the rain halted and the gods hurriedly made their escape. Monkey leapt back down to earth.

The king was about to give Sanzang his permit when Antelope Power stepped forwards. 'Your most August Majesty,' he said. 'For twenty years we Taoists have protected this nation from disaster. We have toiled long and hard preserving this state from drought, famine, war, and other catastrophes. Are you not insulting us by letting these Buddhist monks off the hook just because of some petty magic trick? Please let us challenge them to another competition.'

The king really was muddle-headed; he always agreed with whatever side he had heard last. 'What kind of competition?' he asked.

'Meditation,' replied Antelope Power.

'But these Buddhist monks are masters of meditation,' protested the king.

'The way we practise meditation,' the Immortal replied, 'is not normal. We sit on the tops of great pillars, which we ride up to on clouds. I'm sure we can defeat the monk at that.'

The king put this task before Sanzang, who quickly accepted. 'In my youth,' he said to his disciples, 'a monk of the Chan sect taught meditation at my monastery. I can sit quietly for two or three years.'

'How will we get you to the top of the pillar?' asked Pigsy.

'Simple,' replied Monkey. At this point he left another of his duplicates behind him, and quietly turned his whole body into a cloud. Sanzang quietly stepped onto him and made his ascent to the top of the pillar, just as Tiger Power was doing the same on another pillar.

Both the competitors were skilled at meditation, and the contest had been going for several hours when Deer Power decided to give his brother a hand. He plucked some hairs from his head, rolled them into a ball, and flicked it up at Sanzang's neck, where it immediately turned into a huge louse that began biting and irritating him. The venerable monk was in horrible pain. While his will was enough to keep him still, he desperately wanted to flick the insect off. Monkey began to panic as he saw that his master was close to twitching. Desperate, he decided to go and have a look at Sanzang, knowing that his concentration would be great enough normally to sit on the pillar for decades. With a flick of his hand he transformed into a tiny insect and flew up to his master. Spotting the louse, he quickly flicked it off.

'Monks have bald heads,' thought Monkey, 'so a louse could never settle on one. It must be the doing of those cheating Taoists. Huh! I'll show them cheating.' With this thought Monkey transformed himself into a poisonous centipede, which went straight for Tiger Power's nose. The Taoist could meditate no longer, and fell straight off the pillar. He was saved by his magic cloud, but he had to admit defeat.

The king was about to let the travellers go when Deer Power made a new submission. 'Your Majesty, my brother suffers from rheumatism, and the cold winds up in the air brought on an attack. Please restrain the Buddhists so that I can compete with them in the art of guessing what lies behind wooden boards.'

The foolish king accepted this suggestion, and Sanzang was forced into yet another competition. At first a peach was put into a box. Deer Power stared at this and immediately said 'It is a peach.'

Monkey quickly transformed into an insect again and flew into the box, where he devoured the peach, leaving only the stone. He then flew back to Sanzang and whispered 'Master, say it's only a stone.' Sanzang did indeed repeat this. 'Impossible!' exclaimed the king, 'I put the peach in there myself. The Great Immortal Deer Power is right. Have the Buddhists executed.'

Sanzang immediately jumped in with 'Your Majesty, I am sure it is a stone. Please open the box and have a look.'

The king opened the box and leapt back in astonishment. 'A stone! The monk must have gods or demons on his side.'

Upon hearing this, Pigsy muttered with a sarcastic grin to Sandy, 'He doesn't realize that Monkey is a past master at eating peaches.'

At this point the now-recovered Tiger Power joined in the competition, saying to the king, 'Magic can change only inanimate objects. Put this boy Taoist within the box, and then let the monk guess.' The boy was put in the box, and poor Sanzang was forced to guess yet again what was inside. Monkey was watching the boy as he was put in and began to be a little nervous, knowing he couldn't transform the boy.

Pigsy grinned at Monkey. 'Try and get out of this one, brother. Even you are going to be a bit put off at chomping this little kid down to his bones. It's just as well he's a Taoist, not a Buddhist, or you'd have even more scruples.' Suddenly Pigsy's words gave Monkey an idea. He flew into the box once more, shook himself, and transformed into the exact image of Tiger Power. 'Master!' exclaimed the boy. 'Where have you come from?'

'I am an expert at disappearing magic,' replied Monkey. 'Now, listen closely. The Buddhist saw you being put into the box, and if he guesses right the credibility of our sect is destroyed for ever. We must shave your head and pretend you're a Buddhist monk.'

With this Monkey transformed his cudgel into a razor and instantly shaved the boy's head, as well as transforming his white brocade robe embroidered with flying cranes into a simple brown monk's robe. 'Now, can you chant any sutras?' he asked.

'Master, I know only the Taoist classics,' replied the boy.

'Well then, when you hear the words "There is a monk inside!", come out chanting the name of Amitabha Buddha and save me the trouble of teaching you a sutra. Education nowadays!' sighed Monkey, transforming himself into an insect again.

He then flew out and told Sanzang, 'Master, say "There is a monk inside!"' Sanzang did indeed say this, and the whole court fell back in astonishment as a small Buddhist, with a shaven head and chanting the name of the Buddha climbed out of the chest.

Well, the Taoists were getting desperate by this point. Tiger Power went before the king yet again and said, 'Your Majesty, these Buddhists are skilled indeed. But we have one trick which we feel will defeat them. In our youth, we were taught by a great master certain divine powers. We can put our heads back on after they are cut off, gut ourselves and still live, and take baths in boiling oil. We would like to challenge the Buddhists to these contests.'

Hearing this, bold Monkey exclaimed 'Exactly my line of work! I will happily take on the Great Immortals in these contests.'

Pigsy turned to Monkey and hissed, 'But brother, these are all ways of certain death.'

'You still do not know the full extent of my powers,' replied Monkey.

'You can't have more powers,' cried Pigsy. 'You can already do all of these transformations, and now this! It's not fair!'

Ignoring the moans of the fool Pigsy, Monkey strode up to the execution mound and called for an executioner. He was trussed up like a ball, and his head was laid on the ground. Sanzang was terrified that he would lose his most powerful disciple. He strode up and down nervously – and then stopped as the blade came down. Monkey's head went rolling off and the executioner booted it a good forty feet away. No blood was coming from Monkey's neck as a huge bellow of 'Come back here, head!' arose from his stump of a neck. Tiger Power was so alarmed by this that he ordered the local deities to hold down Monkey's head, so it could not be retrieved by his magic. Monkey was getting worried now, and Sanzang couldn't bear to look, but Pigsy seemed to be enjoying himself at his companion's misfortune.

In frustration, Monkey made the gestures of a spell with his hands and the ropes holding him burst open. He shouted 'Grow!', and, quick as a flash, another head arose from his neck, for he had just as many heads as shapes.

Monkey strolled casually back to his friends, past all the terrified guards. 'Did it hurt?' asked a curious Sanzang.

'Not at all,' replied Monkey. 'It was rather enjoyable, in fact. Haven't done that for years.'

The king thrust their passports at them. 'Take these and go! Go on! Go!' he shouted.

'We're very grateful for the passports,' said Monkey, 'but the Great Immortal hasn't had his turn yet.' Tiger Power was sure he too could perform the same trick, so he strode forward confidently to the mound. His head went flying off, and he too attempted to call it back. Seeing this, Monkey pulled out another of his all-transforming hairs and changed it into a dog, which ran over, seized the Taoist's head by the hair, and dropped it in the palace moat. The Taoist called three times, but, as he had not Monkey's art of growing a new head, his fate was sealed. His headless corpse dropped to the ground, and it was now plain for all to see that he was no man, but instead a yellow-haired tiger.

Deer Power rose to his feet and said 'My elder brother is dead, but he was no tiger. This evil monk has used some trickery. I demand a guts-cutting contest with him.' Cocky Monkey swaggered to the execution ground again. The executioner made a quick cut in his stomach. Monkey thrust his hands into the whole, withdrew his entrails, and began examining them closely. Once he had checked they were all there and whole, he thrust them back in and shouted out 'Grow!' The cut immediately healed up. Monkey walked back to the shocked king, pointed to Deer Power, and, pointing with one thumb at the execution ground, said 'His turn.'

The Immortal strode forward, and began to repeat the same process as Monkey. While he was examining his heart, another of Monkey's hairs was plucked out. Throwing it up in the air, Monkey turned it into a hungry eagle that swept down upon the hapless Taoist, grabbing his entrails and flying off to devour them. Deer Power collapsed to the ground, deprived of all his guts. To everyone's surprise, his body had become that of a white deer.

Antelope Power wailed to the skies and said to the king, 'More evil magic has been used. Please, Your Majesty, let me compete with him in bathing in boiling oil. I will surely defeat him this time.' Two tubs of oil were brought forward, and wood piled underneath them, then set alight. Soon they were bubbling hot. Monkey leapt in as though it was just a normal bath, playing and frolicking around. 'How pleasant,' he said as he turned his gold-banded cudgel into a brush, scratching his back. 'I always find this really is the way to get all the dirt off.' But Monkey shouldn't have been so cocky. In an instant, fuelled by the powers of the Taoists, the flames leapt up. Monkey vanished, consumed by the oil.

Sanzang howled in despair as the Taoists smiled and congratulated Antelope Power. Sandy strode sadly forward to attempt to retrieve the bones of his friend. He glanced into the oil but could see nothing. Pigsy seemed almost to dance as he leapt over to the cauldron. 'Ape!' he shouted. 'Don't have any extra bodies, do you?' He chortled, then peered into the cauldron. 'Ah well,' he said, 'he wasn't much use anyway. Ugly, stupid...'

He got no further as two furry hands grabbed him round the neck. Monkey emerged, furious, from the oil. 'What did you say?' he demanded.

'Monkey!' gasped Sandy, 'What happened?'

'I was joking, that's what happened!' shouted Monkey. 'Does nobody here have a sense of humour?' Sanzang shook his head sadly at the frivolity of his disciple.

Monkey then gestured to Antelope Power. 'Come, my friend. It's your turn for a nice hot bath.' Antelope Power cautiously went forward and got in his bath, going through all the motions of washing himself. Monkey carefully put out a hand, feeling the Immortal's bathing oil. To his surprise, it was cold. 'It looks boiling hot,' he thought. 'One of the dragon kings must be protecting him.' He leapt straight up into the air, where he indeed saw the Dragon King of the Northern Ocean.

'What do you think you're doing, you slimy worm, you scaled slug!' yelled Monkey. 'He's almost equalling me, the beast.' He raised his cudgel threateningly. The dragon king, in fear of Monkey's legendary cudgel, dismissed the cold dragon that had been protecting the Taoist, and swept back quickly to his undersea palace. In an instant the Taoist was quick-fried.

Monkey returned to find the king crying about the loss of his trusted councillors. He slapped him around a bit and said 'Don't be so foolish. Look at those so called Taoists. They were all evil animals who had taken spirit form and come here to destroy you. In a few years they would have overthrown you and taken the kingdom for themselves. Be grateful we appeared to stop them.' At this the king finally came to his senses. He thanked Monkey for aiding him and saving the kingdom, and, at Monkey's prompting, issued a proclamation recalling all monks. When the five hundred were gathered, Monkey made a simple hand sign and all of the hairs flew out from under their nails and reattached themselves to his skin. He then turned to the king, as well as all his subjects and courtiers, who had gathered to see the holy monks, and spoke:

'Now we have defeated these evil beasts you must see there is a Way in the Buddhist teachings also. From now on do not take one religion only, but honour both the Buddhist clergy and the Taoist Way, as well as educating intelligent men following the Confucian fashion. This will make the kingdom secure from evil forever.' The king humbly accepted the wisdom of this advice and kowtowed before the monks, ordering that they should be given all the supplies they wished and escorted out of the kingdom with the greatest honours.

After leaving the Kingdom of Tarrycart, the band experience many dangers, but Monkey's quick wit, Sandy's common sense, and Sanzang's holy simplicity bring them through all their troubles, which mainly revolve around yet more evil flesh-eating demons. Eventually, they arrive at their destination, India.

The End of the Journey

Finally, after many hard years, the small group of travellers came to the West. It was truly a great land of the Buddha. Rare and beautiful flowers bloomed everywhere, ancient trees rose up nearly to the sky, and the air was fresh and crisp like nowhere else they had travelled to. Every family was pious and willingly gave them food. Along the roadside people could be seen meditating on the Buddha's teachings, and sutras could be heard chanted wherever you went. After about a week of journeying through this wondrous place the four friends suddenly came upon a marvellous sight.

Tall buildings rose up into the air, emblazoned with bright colours and covered in sparkling, glittering gemstones. Mystic birds flew about, and fruits of immortality ripened on every tree. Everywhere monks could be seen discussing the sacred Way and chanting the sutras. Sanzang quickly dismounted and went to the gate. From a small postern gatehouse a lay brother called out, 'You must be the Eastern people who have come to collect the scriptures.' Sanzang adjusted his robes and went to meet the gate keeper.

Well, the gatekeeper was certainly no ordinary lay monk. His clothes were golden, and the whisk he carried had a handle of pure jade. Every movement was graceful and elegant, and at his side hung an immortal's tablets. Monkey swiftly nudged Sanzang and whispered 'This is the Gold-crested Immortal who looks after the Jade Truth Temple at the foot of Vulture Peak. He's here to meet us.' Sanzang realized that this must be so and stepped forward to greet him.

'Well,' said the Great Immortal with a smile, 'you certainly took your time to get here. I was told you were going to come about seven years ago.' Pigsy began to mutter about ungrateful Immortals and all the work he'd done for no rewards, but both Monkey and Sandy simultaneously stamped on his toes, causing the idiotic Pigsy to hop about in pain, his complaints forgotten. While this was going on Sanzang was chatting to the Great Immortal, until eventually they were welcomed into the monastery, where they ate, bathed, and eventually dropped off.

The next morning the companions set off to ascend Vulture Peak. As soon as the holy monk Sanzang saw the summit of the Vulture Peak, with beautiful coloured lights shining forth to all directions, he fell to his knees in awe and bowed deeply. 'Master,' said Monkey, 'we're not even at the mountain yet. Don't start bowing right away, or your head will be sore by the time you reach the place.' Sanzang acknowledged the wisdom of this and got up immediately, brushing down his robes.

Once the small group had travelled on a few more miles they reached a vast river. On either side huge waves broke, and the noise was thunderous. 'Monkey,' said the nervous Sanzang, 'what are we going to do? You and the others can leap onto your clouds and cross as easily as I would step across a stream, but there is no bridge, so there is no way for me to cross.'

'Don't worry, don't worry,' said Monkey. 'There's a bridge just over there.'

Sanzang glanced around, and saw a simple sign saying CLOUD-TOUCHING CROSSING, next to a structure that could hardly be called a bridge – it was really no more than a simple log, reaching right across the mighty river. It didn't seem to be quite stable, either, for it often appeared to move slightly in the wind.

Sanzang fell back in alarm. 'There's no way I'm crossing this,' he exclaimed. 'You lot may have mystic powers, but I am only a simple mortal. There's not a chance of me making it safely.'

'Yeah,' said Pigsy, 'Not a chance. Not him nor any of the rest of us. You probably think you can make it, you cocky ape, but you'll be dashed to pieces.'

Laughing, Monkey leapt onto the bridge, and ran nimbly across. 'Come on, Pigsy!,' he shouted.

Pigsy bit at his nails. 'Too hard, too hard,' he moaned, 'I've got a long life ahead of me. I don't want to be drowned in that dreadful torrent.' Monkey ran back across and began to pull at Pigsy, but he struggled with great passion, and Sandy was forced to separate them.

While all this nonsense was going on the venerable monk San-zang spotted a ferryboat. Calling to his disciples to stop arguing, Sanzang began to gesture frantically with his arms until the boat drew closer. With his fiery far-seeing eyes Monkey had already spotted that the ferryman was the Welcoming Lord Buddha, but rather than tell the others he just kept calling.

Eventually the punt drew up, but Sanzang was distressed to see it had no bottom. 'How am I meant to travel in this?' demanded Sanzang.

Monkey calmly replied 'Fear not, master. This boat may be bottomless, but it is more stable than many another boat; it will not capsize even in the middle of a great storm.'

The venerable elder was still doubtful of the veracity of what Monkey said but stepped into the boat nonetheless. Immediately he disappeared into the water. The boatman pulled him out and showed him the trick of standing on the water, while Sanzang shook himself down and complained vehemently about Monkey.

As the boat pushed off a body came floating down the river, to Sanzang's amazement and horror. 'Don't be afraid, master,' said Monkey, 'that's you. You have cast off your worldliness – that's what that body is.'

Pigsy and Sandy immediately began chanting 'It's you! It's you! Congratulations!'

When the boat reached the far side Sanzang turned back to thank the boatman, but found him already gone. It was only after

Monkey had explained the nature of the ferryman that Sanzang understood. He turned to thank his three disciples for all their help in the long and arduous journey, but Monkey refused his thanks, saying 'Master, we've all helped each other. We protected you, and you showed us the way to Enlightenment. We don't deserve your thanks. Now, let's go find the boss.'

As they made their way to Thunder Monastery the wonders of Vulture Peak unfolded before them. Even more splendid than the monastery they had stayed at earlier, Thunder Monastery still palled compared to the natural beauty of the mountain. Immortal apes, picking fruit from rare trees, bowed down to Monkey. Orchids bloomed by the side of the path, and numerous auspicious creatures, including white cranes and phoenixes, could be seen. Eventually the four made their way before the Lord Buddha Tathagata himself, kowtowing in awe at his wondrous presence, even though Monkey still thought he could detect the scent of his own piss on the Buddha's hand. Sanzang humbly presented their request for the scriptures and the Buddha received them with pleasure.

'It has now been fourteen years since you left from the East,' he said, 'seeking to bring the true scriptures to your people. I will willingly grant you the true scriptures that save all beings, for the people of your country are wicked and evil. They do not follow Buddhism, do not turn towards good destinies, and are not patient, righteous, loyal, or kind. In their foolishness and sin they are often reborn as base animals, to feed others with their flesh. They are in sore need of the scriptures, but there are evil-doers and slanderers among them who won't comprehend the full mysteries yet, so I will give you only a portion. Ananda, Kasyapa, fetch these gentlemen a vegetarian meal then present them with a few choice rolls of the scriptures.'

Well, the two Arhats did as commanded. They took the four friends to the storage cupboards, where they found the most essential scriptures for them. But the two Arhats seemed reluctant to hand them over. 'You must have travelled a long way,' said Ananda. 'Did you see any interesting places?'

'Why yes,' replied Sanzang, preparing to launch into a list of their stops.

'Did you pick up anything interesting – I mean, ah, presents,' interrupted Kasyapa.

'Of course not,' said Sanzang. 'We are but simple Buddhist monks.' Ananda and Kasyapa exchanged glances and handed the scriptures over. The small group then left the temple, and prepared to make the long and arduous journey back to the East.

What Sanzang hadn't realized was that the two Arhats, angry at not being bribed properly, had handed over blank scriptures. The Ancient Buddha Dipamkara, overhearing the conversation, had understood immediately. 'Those foolish Chinese,' he thought to himself. 'Imagine accepting worthless scriptures! Ah well, they've travelled a long way, and they deserve something for their pains. I had better fetch them back.' With this he summoned up a divine wind, which rushed after the travellers.

Monkey and his friends had only gone a couple of miles when the divine wind caught up with them. Sanzang smelt the fragrant wind first, but took it only for a good omen. Suddenly the four of them, plus the horse, found themselves whirling round and round in the air, buffeted from side to side. When they finally came down to earth with a bump, the supposed scriptures were scattered all over the ground.

Pigsy ran to pick them up, but exclaimed in a surprised voice, 'Hey, there aren't any words on this scripture!'

Sandy picked up another one and said 'You're right, Brother Pigsy. This one's wordless too, and this one – all of them, in fact!'

'We Easterners are truly unlucky,' cried Sanzang. 'Just when we have the true scriptures in our hands, this wind comes along and blows all the words off!'

'Ahem,' said Monkey, 'Much as I respect your wisdom, master, I don't think that's what actually happened here. What has happened is that those two treacherous Arhats got a bit annoyed after we failed to bribe – give them a present, and gave us false scriptures instead.'

'What are we going to do?' asked Sanzang.

'There's only one thing for it,' said Monkey, gesturing fiercely with his cudgel. 'We're going to have to go back and sort out those two Arhats.'

As it turned out, both Ananda and Kasyapa were very willing to give the true scriptures to the pilgrims without a present. That Monkey had his skull-smashing cudgel waving over both their heads while making comments about how slippery his hands were probably encouraged them a little. Monkey did leave them a cast-off loincloth of his, though, to compensate them for their pains.

Now that Sanzang had transcended his mortal body, the other three found he could cloud-walk along with them, as easily as step along the ground. This made the journey somewhat easier; instead of fourteen years, it took but eight days. Mountains and rivers were avoided with but a single stride, and the journey passed contentedly.

When they arrived in China, Sanzang went straight to the palace of the Emperor Taizong. Taizong, now an ageing man with a grey-tinged beard, rose immediately from his throne.

'Sanzang? You have returned with the scriptures?' Sanzang nodded slowly, a tear of joy running down one cheek.

'You have returned with the scriptures!' the Emperor roared. 'The scriptures have been brought to China! Servants, fetch the finest wine and choice food. We must dine tonight.'

The four companions were toasted across China. Sanzang, having risen above fleshy needs, did not partake of the feast, but Pigsy certainly did, gorging himself in such a foul and disgusting manner that, as the food dribbled down his robes, people wondered if he was a demon the heroes had brought back as a souvenir. He certainly enjoyed himself – and retired to bed full-stomached.

Many tales can be told of how the scriptures were distributed throughout the land, of how a great service was made, or how the wisdom was received by the people. The fate of our heroes, though, is another matter. After the celebrations and festivities were over, Taizong asked Sanzang to read from the scriptures to the court. Sanzang modestly declined, but was pressured into it and climbed on to the podium. As he was about to begin speaking, scented breezes began to waft around him and the Eight Great Vajrapanis appeared behind. Slowly he, along with the other disciples and the white stallion which had borne him for so long, was lifted up into the air. The court gasped in awe and immediately fell to their knees, kowtowing to the great saints who – even if three of them looked like beasts – had brought the sacred scriptures to China.

The final fate of our four friends was, naturally, determined by the Buddha. The companions were brought before him, and the Buddha began to speak.

'Good Monk, in a past life you were a disciple of mine, Master Golden Cicada. But you laughed at my teachings on the Dharna, and lacked respect, so I demoted your soul to be reborn in the East. Now you have learnt my teachings again, and so you are to be made the Candana-Punya Buddha. Monkey, you were crushed by my mountain, and learned my teachings through force rather than acceptance. But you have overcome your evil, and defended this holy monk well throughout his journey. You will be rewarded with high office as the Victorious Fighting Buddha. Pigsy, you used to be a water god at the River of Heaven, but your drunken seduction of an immortal maiden sent you down to Earth as a beast. You sinned greatly before conversion, and your heart is still unregenerate and you are by no means cured of your lust. Still, you bore the baggage well, and so are you to be made Altar-Cleaner.'

'Why are they both Buddhas and I only a lowly Altar-Cleaner?' demanded the unruly Pigsy.

'Because you are fat, lazy, and stupid,' replied the wise Tathagata. 'But Altar-Cleaner for the whole world allows you to chomp plenty of offerings, so your fat belly will be filled. Now, Sandy, you were a Heavenly General till you broke a crystal bowl at an important banquet. You were cast down, but, unlike Pigsy, you have truly reformed, so you will be made the Golden Arhat.' The Buddha then spoke to the white horse. 'You were the son of a Dragon King, but disobeyed your father and were made to carry the holy monk Sanzang as a lowly horse after eating his original one. You bore him well across many dangers, and so you will be made a Heavenly Dragon of the Eight Classes of Being.'

They all kowtowed to show their gratitude, and the horse went down on one knee. As it did so, a mist surrounded it. It gave a great neigh, which slowly turned into a dragon's roar, as it shed the equine form, resuming horns, great golden scales, and a silver beard. Shining all over he flew up into the air, to rejoice in his new-found form. As he did so the migraine-causing band dropped from Monkey's head, and chants rang out throughout Heaven for the two new Buddhas, the Golden Arhat, the Dragon, and, of course, the lowly Altar-Cleaner Pigsy.

STORIES THAT CHANGE THE WORLD

Essential African Mythology

NGANGAR MBITU AND RANCHOR PRIME

African myths reflect the imaginative traditions of hundreds of tribal groups, revealing beliefs about nature, history and the destiny of the world; gods, humanity and society. Some have remained unchanged through generations of storytellers, others are constantly evolving, reflecting the changing culture as tribes meet, traditions mingle and stories merge.

These tales reflect close bonds with the land; everything in nature has its deity or spirit. Some were distant, mighty and mysterious, like the 'sky' god seen in thunder; some entered the individual through spirit possession. Other spirits were seen in the creatures of the tropical forests and the Savannah, which possessed esseentially human traits, for these mythological animals are men and women in different guise. Finally there are myths that tell of the beginning and end of time, how the forces of the cosmos created life, and how the deeds of heroes invented fire and built communities.

Ngangar Mbitu and Ranchor Prime are writers, broadcasters and travellers with a special interest in the myths and legends of Africa, India and Europe. They have worked on educational and environmental research projects and are members of Icorec.

Essential Russian Mythology

PYOTR SIMONOV

The variety and colour of Russian myths are as wide-ranging as the country of Russia itself. Legends tell of the arrival many centuries ago of the first Slavs, who formed close bonds with the rivers and fertile land that fed and protected them. This became the Moist Earth of their myths, alive with spirits and mysterious forces that came to govern their pattern of life. As the Slavs spread through Russia, moving across unknown mountains and barren steppes, their stories were shaped by the world they saw, the spirits they sensed and the formidable heroes they encountered.

These myths are so intricately woven into the oral traditions of the people that even with the arrival of Christianity they were not lost. One legend tells how the mighty Prince Vladimir wiped out the old gods in person, but could not wipe them out from the memory of the people. Their wonders and deeds live on in the new faith through the epic tales and folklore which are retold here.

Pyotr Simonov has travelled extensively throughout Russia and Eastern Europe. A Byzantine scholar, he is particularly interested in the links between traditional Russian culture and ecology, and is currently working on ways to revive traditional methods of farming in Russia. He is a member of Icorec.

Essential Celtic Mythology

LINDSAY CLARKE

Celtic legends, with their romance and violent struggles, capture the spirit of the ancient Celts of Ireland and Wales. These tales of mighty battles fought by warrior kings, of events that trace the rise and fall of kingdoms, are rich with the magic and mystery that is woven into the lives of their people.

Reaching back to a time when the people of the Earth-goddess Danu ruled Ireland, these oral tales handed down through genera-tions tell of the land and of remote tribes conquered by the Celts. They tell of painful battles against the giants of the deep sea, the Fomors; of the magic power of spells, the tricks of hidden spirits and leprechauns; the awesome temperament of the natural world; the power and enchantment of love and revenge. Recounted here by Lindsay Clarke, these myths draw the reader into the world of the Celts, and their history and traditions that have resonated through the ages to the present day.

Lindsay Clarke, author of *Chymical Wedding* and *Alice's Masque* and winner of the 1989 Whitbread Prize for Fiction, is one of Britain's best known novelists. He has extensive knowledge of mythology and legend and runs workshops in the UK and abroad.

Essential African Mythology	1 85538 478 7	£6.99	☐
Essential Russian Mythology	1 85538 475 2	£6.99	☐
Essential Celtic Mythology	1 85538 477 9	£6.99	☐

All these books are available from your local bookseller or can be ordered direct from the publishers.

To order direct just tick the titles you want and fill in the form below:

Name: _____

Address: _____

_____

_____

Postcode: _____

Send to: Thorsons Mail Order, Dept 3, HarperCollins*Publishers*, Westerhill Road, Bishopbriggs, Glasgow G64 2QT.

Please enclose a cheque or postal order or your authority to debit your Visa/Access account —

Credit card no: _____

Expiry date: _____

Signature: _____

— up to the value of the cover price plus:

UK & BFPO: Add £1.00 for the first book and 25p for each additional book ordered.

Overseas orders including Eire: Please add £2.95 service charge. Books will be sent by surface mail but quotes for airmail dispatches will be given on request.

24-HOUR TELEPHONE ORDERING SERVICE FOR ACCESS / VISA CARDHOLDERS — TEL: 0141 772 2281